FLY-FISHING FOR PIKE

FLY-FISHING *for* PIKE

David Wolsoncroft-Dodds

PERTH & KINROSS COUNCIL	
05702283	
Bertrams	28/07/2012
799.175	£25.00
AKB	

Quiller

First published in the UK in 2010
by Quiller, an imprint of Quiller Publishing Ltd

British Library Cataloguing-in-Publication Data
A catalogue record for this book
is available from the British Library

ISBN 978 1 84689 054 3

Design and typesetting by Paul Saunders

All photographs in Chapter 4 by Sebastian Wolsoncroft-
Dodds, other photographs by the author, except where
stated: all photographs copyright of the photographer.

Printed in China

Quiller

An imprint of Quiller Publishing Ltd
Wykey House, Wykey, Shrewsbury, SY4 1JA
Tel: 01939 261616 Fax: 01939 261606
E-mail: info@quillerbooks.com
Website: www.countrybooksdirect.com

CONTENTS

Author's Note

Living in Wiltshire, in England, I do most of my fishing in Great Britain and Ireland, with occasional, highly welcome, sorties to Scandinavia and Canada. This being so, most of the references within these pages are to fishing in these regions – and, being a fairly traditional Englishman, I have given measurements of rods, line, weights of fish and so on in imperial units. (Regarding this second point, I have to own up to the fact that a 22 lb pike sounds bigger than one of 10 kg!) These apparent parochialisms notwithstanding, I hope that this book will be of interest and value to anglers in all countries that harbour the wonderful, sporting pike.

INTRODUCTION

M Y JOURNEY TO FLY-FISHING for pike started many years ago. As a young lad, long before I had become familiar with a fly-rod, I dragged the odd jack out of a nearby lake. This was achieved with my uncle's carp rod, which I used to hurl out a silver bar-spoon. There was no great skill attached to this. Every now and then a small pike would grab the lure and I would be faced with the awkward task of removing the oversized, cruelly barbed treble hooks. Over the years, I became absorbed in the mystery that is fly-fishing for trout, sea trout and salmon. From April to October, I enjoyed this sport. I was, after all, fishing for the finest fish using the most demanding and fascinating method. During the cold, dark months of the winter, I still needed to feel a bend in my rod, so I fished for pike.

I used my trusty Hardy salmon-spinning rod and an Abu multiplier. Mostly, I fished with plugs or spinners but when the water was coloured, I resorted to fishing with herrings or other fish baits. It wasn't as satisfying or as entertaining as fly-fishing but it was better than not fishing.

In many ways, it was akin to methadone – a way of managing my addiction. When, eventually, I realised that I could fish for pike with a fly-rod, the cure gradually became the disease. It was a realisation that came in stages. First, I got to grips with handling tackle that enabled me to cast what I then considered large flies. (I would now consider these early attempts at pike-flies to be quite diminutive.)

▲ A perfect morning on a perfect, natural lake – it doesn't get much better. The morning sun has burnt off the mist and we've found the pike. I'm connected to a good fish that took my fly high in the water. Richard Morrish and I enjoyed great sport as the pike hammered a shoal of perch.
(*Richard Morrish*)

I caught pike, my confidence grew and my addiction intensified. I made progress largely through my own endeavours. There was little available in terms of literature to learn from and no seasoned local expert to offer me guidance. I came to regard pike as more rewarding quarry than fat, farmed rainbow trout. I also came to regard pike as more exciting quarry than even the wiliest wild brown trout. Pike also gave me a more realistic chance of a big fish on a fly-rod than did the lordly salmon – at least they were readily available in England. They offered encouragement. By improving my skills and by developing my knowledge, I was rewarded with success.

Fly-fishing for pike has now become an all-consuming obsession. When I'm not pursuing pike for my own pleasure, I'm writing about it or guiding and teaching other anglers. I no longer cry-off when faced with unfavourable conditions. Rather, I have worked to develop techniques (and borrowed some from other anglers) which allow me to catch pike consistently, throughout the year.

Whether I'm revelling in the excitement of fishing surface poppers on a calm June morning or tweaking a bomber close to the bottom of the lake on a cold, dark day in January, I fish with confidence. I'm prepared to accept that, on some days, the bait-fisher may catch more pike than me – on some days, yes, but not on many days.

The ability to fish my fly enticingly, combined with a mobile, searching approach that sees me covering the right parts of the water, means that I now catch a lot of pike every year.

A friend relayed to me a conversation he'd had with a lure fisherman in his local tackle shop. This fisherman had agreed that fly-fishing for pike would be fun but he thought it would only catch small fish. Nothing could be further from the truth. I've caught many, many pike over 20 lb, as have several of my guiding clients. I've caught eight pike of more than 30 lb with my fly-rod and two of my clients have landed a 'big thirties'.

I've discovered that the techniques I have developed, fishing my local waters in rural Wiltshire, have proved just as viable in many other countries. I have even caught pike from the sea, fishing the Swedish Archipelago in the Baltic. I think that the fly can be so effective because it can be fished slowly and teasingly and in a way that is sufficiently lifelike to trigger a feeding response.

Apart from the fact that fly-fishing for pike can be successful in terms of numbers and size of pike caught, it's also supremely enjoyable and satisfying. You travel light, hunting the pike where they live, rather than enticing them to you. Fly-fishing for pike is more an art-form than a mere technique. I have

◄ When a pike hits your fly, in full view, high in the water, it sends your pulse into overdrive.
(Andy Bowman)

▲ When you have enjoyed catching a pike, it's important to ensure that the fish is returned quickly and carefully. I'm supporting this Irish pike until it can swim away strongly. *(Andy Bowman)*

come to accept its limitations, which I impose on myself voluntarily. I'm rewarded with the special pleasure that comes from seeing a hefty pike hit the accurately cast fly that I have tied myself and feeling every surge and pull as she tries to show me who's the boss! (Since all big pike are females, I've referred to them as such throughout this book. Apart from being factually correct, I think that this 'personalising' heightens the respect I feel for these awesome creatures.)

A pike caught on a fly tied on a big, barbless single hook can fight far harder than one with a mouthful of treble hooks that's handicapped by having to drag a float and weights around.

All this doesn't mean that I'm impervious to the pleasure that can come from fishing for other species with a fly-rod. I still cast a fly for wild brown trout in April when the pike are spawning. If I'm in Scotland or Ireland and there are salmon in the river, I may take a day out to enjoy the relaxation of Spey-casting. In the dog-days of high summer when the pike are dull and lethargic, on the right day, I'll head for the north Devon coast and I'll enjoy catching some jet-propelled, silvery bass.

However, these infidelities are mere casual affairs. I'm locked into an enduring and blossoming relationship with a demanding mistress. The pike, especially the big, female pike are an inspiring challenge. They are dominant, at the top of the food chain, savage mistresses of their domain. I don't claim to understand every facet of their behaviour. Sometimes I'm frustrated by them, but always, I'm intrigued. I hope, in the chapters which follow, to convey something of my enthusiasm and to encourage you in your endeavours to catch pike with a fly-rod.

Throughout this book, I will employ some rather woolly terminology. Words such as usually, generally and normally, will abound. I learned many years ago that pike have their own agenda. They are too capricious for us to try to apply strict rules and certainties to them. Over the years, the more that I have learned, the more I have come to appreciate how much more there is to be learned. I don't intend to cut short my education.

Chapter 1

GETTING STARTED

MANY TROUT FISHERMEN, thinking about venturing into fly-fishing for pike, are racked by a crisis of confidence. They perceive that there are too many obstacles to overcome and too many problems to face. They worry at the prospect of casting large pike flies – after all, it was difficult enough to learn to cast trout flies. They worry about handling a big, lively fish with a head full of teeth. (This worry is often exacerbated by the experience of accidentally catching a pike on a trout fly and being totally unprepared.) They realise that, for any given volume of water, there will be fewer pike than trout. Obviously, pike are at the pinnacle of the freshwater food chain so are heavily outnumbered by their food supply. This could make pike difficult to locate and catch.

The answer is simple. As pike fly-fishers, we have to journey beyond simply mastering the mechanical aspects of fly-fishing. We have to connect with our quarry and the environment the pike inhabit. Some of the large waters that are famous for huge pike can seem intimidating. Irish loughs such as Mask, Derg and Corrib – even English trout reservoirs such as Chew – are on an altogether different scale from commercial trout fisheries. Understanding the seasonal rhythms of the water and how the pike react to them is important for our success and adds to our pleasure. We can learn the skills required and use our watercraft to refine our tactics and narrow down our searches.

▶ Many fly-fishers are somewhat nervous at the prospect of handling pike. This 20 lb fish, which I caught on opening day from an old estate lake, has an impressive set of jaws. When you learn how to hold your fish properly, you won't have any problems and will be able to deal with pike safely and with confidence.
(Richard Morrish)

Big waters soon become less intimidating when we apply our knowledge to them. Learning to handle a boat enables us to explore the whole of the pikes' territory. We don't have to start by fishing waters that are beyond our fledgling skills. Rather, we can learn as we progress and we can enjoy the unfolding adventure that is fly-fishing for pike.

Most coarse fishermen find the prospect of learning to cast a fly daunting. They think it will prove a difficult skill to master. Their view is that they can already catch pike by dead-baiting – so why make it more difficult? They are also prey to various misconceptions. Many assume that fly-fishing for pike is merely a 'fun method' occasionally dabbled in by television celebrities taking a break from the serious business of catching big pike. There is the thought that fly-fishing is comparatively unproductive and will only produce the occasional pike. There is the additional assumption that these pike will be smaller fish. Many coarse fishermen have become convinced that big pike are mere scavengers rather than hunters. Believe me, this isn't the case. The biggest pike that I have ever seen charged at and engulfed my fly. I made a complete hash of trying to connect with her. Seeing such a huge fish hit my fly completely wrecked my nervous system. I struck too quickly and merely splatted my fly into my wading jacket.

I nowadays expect to catch more than 400 pike in a year, which hardly makes fly-fishing unproductive. Every year, this total will include a number of pike weighing more than 20 lb and some years it will include fish of more than 30 lb. This hardly qualifies as tiddler-snatching. I don't possess supernatural powers – fly-fishing for pike works!

Some coarse fishermen, on discovering the cost of the most expensive fly-rods, are frightened off by the apparently high price of equipment and gain the false impression that fly-fishing is the sole preserve of the wealthy. Now, it is true that 'cheap and nasty' stuff is false economy (this applies to coarse gear as well) and it is also true that, given the rigours of fly-fishing for pike, it makes sense to obtain the best tackle one can reasonably afford, but there is plenty of sensibly priced, serviceable gear available. (This issue is discussed in more detail in the next chapter.)

Of these misconceptions that apply to coarse fishermen, certainly, the biggest hurdle to be overcome is the false perception that casting with a fly-rod is an arcane skill that can only be mastered by a few individuals with enormous natural talent – and only then after many years of practice. Take heart! I had decidedly average natural ability; I now demonstrate casting pike flies at game fairs and fly-fishing shows. This has come about by putting some effort into understanding the mechanics of casting big flies, a few hours coaching, some practice in the park and – most enjoyably – lots of pike fishing.

Whether you are a coarse fisherman looking for a new and more challenging way of catching a quarry you are familiar with or an aspirant fly-fisherman looking for a new and challenging quarry, you need to learn how to cast pike flies. It would be foolish of me to suggest that this can be achieved in a single hour. However, it is an eminently learnable skill. I often equate it with learning to drive and, as with learning to drive, most individuals benefit from professional instruction. I would suggest that you enlist the help of an instructor for, at least, a couple of lessons.

Take care with choosing your instructor and check that he understands what you are looking to achieve. Many well-qualified casting instructors are only familiar with casting small trout flies and assume that the techniques required for this will simply 'scale up' for larger flies. This isn't so. If you struggle to find a suitable teacher, contact me (see contact details in the Appendix) and I will connect you to someone in your area who can help.

You can also benefit from going fishing with an experienced pike fly-fisher. This can be particularly useful for trout fishermen who are nervous about handling pike. Again, take care with choosing a mentor. Many people who have fly-fished for pike for several years have ingrained bad habits and have never learned to cast properly. However, the vast majority of my own guiding

▲ Learning to cast big pike flies effectively is crucial to your enjoyment of the sport. Mark Corps, pictured here making a long, relaxed cast on an Irish lough, is a qualified, expert instructor. A few casting lessons can prove a worthwhile investment and can ensure that you don't acquire bad habits. *(Andy Bowman)*

clients have become regular or dedicated pike fly-fishermen and many would be happy to take a beginner under their wing. If you are looking for such a mentor, then, as with casting instruction, contact me and I will put you in touch with someone suitable in your part of the country.

All experienced pike anglers – whatever their preferred techniques – would agree that it's important that you get to know the water you are fishing. Because of this, I would recommend starting your pike fly-fishing on a relatively small water. (Although, if you are lucky enough to live on the shores of Loch Lomond or Lough Mask, then feel free to ignore this advice!) It's also a good idea to pick a water that is close to home. The more you can fish a venue, the more quickly you will build up an understanding of it. I was fortunate to start my pike fly-fishing on an old estate lake that I had fished for several winters with my now redundant spinning rod. It provided the perfect introduction as the pike fishing was excellent and I already knew something about the venue. I enjoyed some early success which boosted my confidence and gave me the motivation to continue.

A visit to your local fishing tackle dealer should help you to identify some suitable waters. It's worth visiting a few. Many coarse fisheries hold good pike but aren't really fishable with a fly-rod. They may have limited bank access and have no space behind for your back-cast. Nevertheless, anyone in England, living outside the urban sprawl, will have good pike fishing close to hand. Many rivers provide first-class, productive pike fishing. This fishing is often very affordable – I have two stretches of river on my doorstep which cost the miserly sum of £30 for a full season. Many rivers such as these run through beautiful, unspoilt countryside and are relatively neglected as so many people prefer to fish small, artificial commercial fisheries which are overstocked and offer unrealistically easy fishing.

In addition to visiting the tackle shop, talk to members of your local fishing clubs. You will find them more than willing to help. Carry out as much research on your 'starter waters' as possible, but resist the urge to fish too many waters. You are more likely to achieve some confidence-building success if you restrict your efforts to a few venues. Good results come from building up your knowledge.

The best time to start fly-fishing for pike is the post-spawning period. This is when pike are reasonably easy to locate and are most likely to hit your fly with enthusiasm. It's also the time (usually!) when the weather gods are at their most benign. For most anglers in England, this means a start date of 16 June, although some trout reservoirs will let you fly-fish for pike which means that you can start in May, when the pike have recovered from their spawning efforts. However, these reservoirs are generally big expanses of water and if you aren't happy about handling a boat, this may make it difficult to locate pike. If you live in Scotland or Ireland, there is no statutory close season for pike, just a self-imposed one, to let them spawn in peace.

If you are not familiar with fly-casting from a boat, start off by picking a venue you can fish from the bank. It's easier to learn to cast big pike flies when you have got solid ground under your feet. Bank fishing also makes a short session a sensible option. Normally, if I have taken the trouble to launch my boat or hire one, then I am fishing for the whole day. (Also, to start with, you may find casting pike flies for a full day too much like hard work. When you have developed a sound, relaxed casting style, this problem will be a thing of the past.)

When you decide to take up the challenge of fly-fishing for pike, it is important to understand that you will be fishing for a wild quarry. They don't gobble anything you throw at them, in the manner of recently stocked, farmed fish.

On some days, they will frustrate you. On some days, you will get it wrong. You will be in the wrong place at the wrong time. I'll readily admit that I experience some blank sessions every year. Pike, even big, well educated specimens, haven't read this book and can sometimes be aggravatingly unpredictable. Sometimes, you can do everything right but be faced with pike that indulged in a feeding frenzy yesterday and just can't be persuaded to take your fly. Pike fishing is a demanding sport. It isn't as straightforward as catching suicidal, stockie rainbows from an overpopulated pond.

▶ Pike are wild fish and live in wild places. This hefty one, connected to Andy Bowman's rod, became decidedly wild when close to the boat! She made several long, powerful runs before I was able to net her safely.

This doesn't make it less enjoyable – far from it! Whilst you need to accept that on some days you will struggle, you will also get the chance to experience some real, red-letter days. A four-fish limit catch from a commercial trout fishery just doesn't compare with a dozen good-sized pike in a session. Catches like this may not be the norm but they do happen. If you fly-fish for pike regularly, it will happen for you – every year. Pike grow big. If you elect to fish waters where big pike live, and if you fish regularly, you will catch some – every year. In my opinion, a 20 lb pike, caught on a fly-rod, is every bit as satisfying as landing a good salmon. Fly-fishing also teaches you to value the smaller pike. For the dead-baiter, a 5 lb jack pike can be an anticlimax. For the fly-fisher, deceiving that same fish so that it takes your carefully crafted, roach-imitating fly is a special pleasure. The visual excitement of seeing that same fish hit the fly high in the water never palls.

Fly-fishing for pike can also take you to some stunningly beautiful places. My local waters are fabulous – far more appealing than neatly sanitised commercial fisheries. Scottish lochs, surrounded by impressive high hills, are a delight to visit. I particularly enjoy the wild limestone loughs of Ireland where there is always the chance of a pike to compare with the mythical monsters of old. Canada (for those who can afford it) offers the chance to experience genuine wilderness fishing on a grand scale. Because we can fly-fish for pike for most of the year, we can really connect with the natural environment. Because we can fish for pike in a wide variety of venues, we can enjoy mastering a wide range of techniques. This means that when you take up the challenge of fly-fishing for pike, you can look forward to many years of developing your know-ledge and skills.

Many anglers like the idea of the support that belonging to a club can provide. The Pike Fly-fishing Association and The Pike Anglers Club of Great Britain can be useful sources of information and encouragement. I have listed their contact details, along with many other useful contacts, in the Appendix at the end of the book.

Every journey starts with a single step. Learn to cast. Get properly equipped. Set out on your own adventure.

Chapter 2

TACKLE

M ANY FLY-FISHERS WILL start their pike fly-fishing by using equipment
that they already have. Certainly a 7 or 8 weight reservoir trout rod can
be used to catch the odd pike. However, as you have taken the trouble to buy
this book, I am assuming that you don't want to 'make do' but would rather be
properly equipped for the job.

I have covered the choice of flies in the next chapter. The smallest fly that
I normally use is 6 in (15 cm) long, tied on a wide gape, 4/0 hook. Flies as big
as this demand the use of suitable specialist equipment. As with all fly-fishing,
it is essential that our tackle is balanced to allow us to achieve the best possible
performance.

Rods

I'll start with rods, as these are the items that most fly-fishers are obsessed with.
Rods for fly-fishing for pike are generally 9 ft (3 m) long and rated at 9 or 10
weight. Several years ago, I used a 9 weight rod most of the time and landed
my biggest pike of over 30 lb on one. I now find myself using larger flies and as
my flies have grown, I now use a 10 weight rod for most of my fishing. There are
a few rods marketed specifically for fly-fishing for pike. However, most of the
rods we have to choose from are really designed as saltwater models. The

explosion of interest in fly-fishing for hard-fighting, sea fish means that we now have a good range of models from which to select.

Because I do a lot of fishing and help many guiding clients, I own more fly-rods than any man should. They all have different characteristics which suit them to specific situations and particular individuals.

My personal choice for a high percentage of my pike fly-fishing is a Hardy Zane 10 weight. This is a powerful rod with a crisp, fast action, which lets me cast big flies a long way. It has enough 'grunt' in the butt to allow me to put pressure on big, hard-fighting fish. It also has the robust build-quality to stand up to the rigors of pike fishing. However, it needs the right line to wake it up and wouldn't be to everyone's taste. Some of my guiding clients with limited casting expertise fare better with a more forgiving rod. Many top-notch pike fly-fishers prefer rods that aren't as stiff. I, too, have a rod with an all-through, progressive action. It loads easily and is perfect for short range work on smaller rivers and for belly-boating. It's also an ideal rod for someone new to the mysteries of double-haul casting.

A top quality fly-rod manufactured by one of the famous brands (Hardy, Sage, Orvis, G Loomis et al.) can put a fair dent in your wallet (around £600 in

▼ A pike fly-rod has to be much more than a casting machine. I'm trying to stop a hefty Irish pike from powering down into the ranunculus on a steep drop-off. *(Andy Bowman)*

2008). I know many pike fly-fishers of very modest means who have scrimped and saved to buy their perfect rod. I, in fact, have used rods that I paid more for than the battered car I drove to the lake. As I mentioned in the previous chapter, many coarse anglers are alarmed when they see the price of the highest-quality fly-fishing equipment, and then assume that fly-fishing is the preserve of the wealthy. (One fact they often ignore at this point is that they themselves tend to buy many rods, reels, gadgets and accessories such as bite alarms and have a bait bill every time they go out to the water. Fly-fishing is an altogether more minimalist affair!) Fortunately, however, there are also many perfectly serviceable rods which don't inflict too much damage on one's finances. That said, I would always be wary of buying a truly cheap rod, since this may prove to be a false economy. A rod which doesn't perform and which you aren't happy with won't save you money – you'll simply consign it to a jumble sale and buy a new one.

Fly-fishing for pike puts a huge amount of stress on a rod, and a high percentage of my guiding clients have had rods break whilst fishing. (The more expensive fly-rods usually have 'original owner' lifetime warranties, but although this may provide some peace of mind, it doesn't help if you break your only rod on day one of your week-long expedition to a remote Irish lough.) The stresses come from casting bulky flies and dealing with heavyweight, explosive fighting fish at close quarters. Some rods perform perfectly well if they aren't subjected to these stresses but don't measure up for pike fishing.

It will be evident from this that choosing your rod is a serious undertaking. The right choice will provide you with many years of good service and pleasure. The wrong choice will be a waste of your hard-earned cash. Don't just visit your nearest fly-fishing emporium and walk out with the rod the salesman wants you to buy. Don't be dazzled by a review and send off your payment to the company that sent you a glossy catalogue. I am constantly amazed at how many people will buy a rod without trying it first. If you are using a guide or instructor, he should have a variety of rods for you to experiment with. Visit the fly-fishing shows or game fairs and give some rods a thorough workout. Take a realistically large dummy pike-fly. A rod that feels fine with the salesman's so called pike-fly can be much less impressive when connected to a 7 in double bunny that has absorbed a gallon of water.

Whilst I regard a single-handed rod as the quintessential fly-fishing tool, I do sometimes find a two-handed, long salmon rod can let me fish waters where I would struggle to manage with my normal 9-footer. This applies particularly to stretches of my local rivers, which haven't been neatly manicured for fly-fishing. A double-hander lets me explore areas with high banks and extensive marginal reed growth. It also allows me to handle my fly, mend the line and work eddies and slacks that would prove difficult with a conventional rod. The extra length compensates for the fact that I can't double-haul with a two-handed rod. I certainly don't suggest that everyone should dash out and buy a top of the range Spey-casting rod for their pike fishing. However, if you are a salmon fisher and have such a rod sitting in your tackle room, it can give you some unexpected extra entertainment. It can also let you fish in some unspoilt places which offer productive pike fishing.

If, like most anglers, you are going to choose a single rod for your pike fly-fishing, make it a 9 ft, single-handed 9 or 10 weight. Pick a rod with a fast action but not so fast that you find it difficult to cast with. To describe the ideal rod in motoring terms, it should be as robust as an agricultural tractor with the performance of a Porsche. Buy the best rod that you can afford. Get to know it – hopefully it will be at the heart of many wonderful fishing memories for you. Another point – it's a good idea to pick a rod that comes in four sections. When packed in its protective tube, it will stow in your suitcase and can be part of your luggage if you are jetting off to far-flung places. Modern technology has meant that such rods have actions that are every bit as sweet as two-piece models.

Many fishermen who use 'conventional' techniques for pike assume that because a fly-rod is more flexible than the rods they use to hurl out whole fish-baits, it won't be powerful enough to subdue a heavyweight pike. They assume that the fly-fisher will cause the pike unnecessary stress by playing it for too long. Nothing could be further from the truth. Sure, my fly-rod is often bent into an alarming horseshoe shape by a big pike. I don't get alarmed – that's the whole idea! I am confident that my rod will perform. A 9 or 10 weight fly-rod allows you put a lot of pressure on a pike and its flexibility makes it a perfect cushion against the heart-stopping, arm-wrenching runs that a powerful pike will make. I land big pike just as quickly as the bait-fisher and have a lot more fun in the process!

Reels

On the face of it, choosing a reel shouldn't be quite such an involved process as choosing a rod. In fact, there is a body of opinion that relegates a fly-reel to a mere device for storing the line. Pike have convinced me that this is a dangerous philosophy.

The first requirement of a reel for pike fly-fishing is that it should be big enough to hold a couple of hundred yards of 30 lb backing and store the heavy fly-line without the coils being too tight. This rules out using a trout reel. Most salmon reels will meet this requirement but they are usually made to match with double-handed Spey rods and are a bit too heavy to balance sweetly with a 9 ft, single-handed rod (more so if you are using a 9 weight rather than a 10 weight). At first sight, the need for two hundred yards of backing may seem a bit over the top. Although pike can fight very hard and make many runs, they are not renowned for making long runs. However, whilst this is true on most waters, gin-clear loughs with deep water close by can be a very different pro-position. I've had several big pike power off on interminable runs as they have tried to reach the other end of the lake. Andy Smith, of the Hardy Instructors Academy, has had similar experiences when fishing gravel pits where the water has been crystal clear.

As with rods, many reels that match our requirements have been designed as saltwater models. Manufacturers such as Hardy, Abel and Tibor make beau-tifully engineered masterpieces that will give many years of faithful service and are a delight to own. Inevitably, top of the range saltwater reels don't come

▼ If you fish where big pike live, you want a robust reel with a smooth, reliable drag system. These models are both large enough to store the fly-line without it being crammed onto the spool in tight coils. They are also able to house enough backing line to cope with a pike that decides to head for the middle of the lake. *(Andy Bowman)*

cheaply. Often spare spools for these reels are also expensive. As you progress with your pike fly-fishing, it's likely that you will want extra spools to house different lines to allow you to fish with a range of techniques. Often, too, changing spools on these saltwater models can be a fiddly process – not easily accomplished with numb fingers on an icy January morning.

A few years ago, I had a top of the range reel for most of my fishing and bought a more economical model, with correspondingly cheaper spare spools, as a back-up and to handle a variety of line options. There is now an altogether more satisfactory solution available. Hardy's Demon is a high-quality reel, machined from aerospace aluminium. Spare spools are made from a plastic composite material and slot neatly into the structure of the reel. The result is a perfect combination of quality and value for money. In the past, cartridge-type reels had been aimed at the lower end of the market. I liked the idea of the Demon but was reserving judgement until I had tangled with a pike that would give the drag a real battle. After landing a fish in Ireland that tried to convince me it was a barracuda, I no longer have any misgivings. (Knowing how rapidly developments take place in the fishing tackle industry, I'm sure that other manufacturers will produce high-quality cartridge reels to expand the choice available to pike fly-fishers.)

I've read that a reel with a good drag isn't necessary for pike fishing. Often, you can play a pike with your 'spare' hand controlling the fly-line you have retrieved and without bringing the reel into action. A while ago, I was fishing a favourite old estate lake near my home. The day was cold and miserable, with the wind driving drizzly rain into every gap it could find in my clothing. I'd been casting and retrieving my fly for many hours and had reached the point where I was fishing mechanically with no real hope of a take. I put out a long line to take my fly past the drop-off. Before I had tightened to my fly, there was a huge swirl on the surface. The fly-line was pulled out of my numb-fingered grip and shot through my rings. My rod bowed, my reel purred, my leader held – the battle was on. Ten minutes later, I brought a 24 lb pike over the net. It could have been horribly different. Had my drag yielded line too readily, the speed and weight of the fish could easily have caused the reel to overrun. The resulting 'bird's nest', jamming in my butt ring, would have left me with a snapped leader. Had my drag not yielded line smoothly, with no start-up inertia, my leader would have broken like a strand of cotton. In such circumstances a reliable drag isn't a luxury! If you fish waters that contain big pike, at some point you will connect with one. When you do, you will want to feel confident that your tackle is totally trustworthy.

Whichever reel you select, fit it (loaded with line and backing) to your rod before you part with your cash. It's important that the combination feels comfortable in your hand.

Line

Most anglers pay close attention to choosing their rod and reel. However, selecting the right fly-line is, without question, the most important choice we have to make when assembling our tackle for fly-fishing for pike.

My early efforts were unsuccessful, frustrating and wasted both time and money. I tried using lines designed for salmon fishing. I struggled. Rather than the neat, tight loops I had been used to generating when casting trout flies, I found myself trying to cope with something that resembled a strand of over-cooked spaghetti waggling around at the end of my rod. When Spey-casting, I had been accustomed to having about twenty yards of line on the water. When pike fishing, I was retrieving the fly to my toes and trying to start a cast with just a few inches of line outside my tip-ring. I horrified my local tackle dealer by taking a pair of scissors to proprietary fly-lines, although my efforts at re-engineering lines did improve matters.

Nowadays, such measures are unnecessary – we have some first-class lines available and there are some fly-lines on the market aimed specifically at the pike angler. Some of these are very good – Rio and Courtland have excellent pike fly-lines. The lines I currently use most often are Rio Outbound Coldwater lines and I have clients who favour the 'short head' versions of these particular lines. On the other hand, some fly-lines intended for pike are next to useless and will cause much frustration.

Because we are casting large flies, the line needs to be a weight forward design, with a short, bullet taper head (the heavier part of the line, which loads the rod for casting). This style of line will get the rod working with the minimum of fly-line through the tip ring and will turn over the fly. That said, different rods with different actions will be suited by different lines. My fast-action rod needs a line with a shorter, heavier head than do my more forgiving rods.

Thus, the crucial consideration when choosing a line is balance. The line must load your rod properly and turn over the fly you are using, so that you can cast smoothly and effectively. With rods and reels, you may decide to compromise between cost, quality and performance. With lines, only the very best will do. The most expensive rod and reel combination will be rendered useless if teamed with an unsuitable line. Properly balanced, your pike fly-rod will feel like an extension of your forearm and will give you enormous pleasure. Many beginners find casting pike flies hard, physical work. This is because they put far too much effort into the process – it's far better to perfect your casting technique and fine-tune your tackle.

The importance of getting the line right has been illustrated for me by clients who have come to me for help. Some of these clients have been anglers who have been confident enough of their skills when casting trout flies but have felt completely feeble and inadequate when casting big pike flies. Often, their line wouldn't load their rod and had too gentle a taper to turn over the larger flies and form an aerodynamic casting loop. On several occasions, the casting lesson, booked for two hours, has lasted twenty minutes. The client, with perfectly sound technique, has realised that his problem was one of tackle selection rather than casting skill and has left a happy and wiser man.

As with rods and reels, many of the lines we can choose from for fly-fishing for pike are designed as saltwater tackle. Beware! The line marketed for tarpon fishing may perform faultlessly in the spring and summer. However, when the weather and the water cool, you may find yourself trying to cast with something that resembles coils of fence wire! Some saltwater lines are for tropical

▼ Rod, reel and line need to be in harmony. Correctly balanced tackle makes casting a relaxed pleasure and enables you to achieve optimum performance without making it hard work. (Gardiner Mitchell)

use. When selecting lines for pike fishing, we need to choose ones with cold-water coatings.

I use a floating line for the majority of my pike fishing. Many experienced and successful anglers use intermediate or sinking lines as their first choices. This is less an argument about the most useful line and more a question of the waters we fish and how we fish them. I tend to fish natural waters more often than man-made trout reservoirs, and I often fish from the bank or wade, rather than fish from a boat. Whilst the floating line is the one I'll use most often in the year, I'll use a whole range of lines to allow me to fish my fly in the way I want to. This means that I'll employ sink-tips, intermediates, slow-sinking and high-density, fast-sinking lines.

On occasion, I also use shooting heads. These are short lengths of full weight fly-lines which are attached to finer running lines. You can buy proprietary versions but I'll often make my own by trimming the head section of an old salmon line. These can be particularly useful for constructing high-density lines which will sink a buoyant fly. Shooting heads can also help with casting very large (12 in) flies.

Don't panic! I'm not suggesting that you need a full armoury of lines before you can fly-fish for pike. If you start your campaign in the spring, you will probably only need a floating line. The addition of an intermediate after you have caught some pike will cover most situations. The reasons why I now use a full range of lines are because I do a huge amount of pike fishing, on a wide variety of waters, and am always looking to get the best possible performance and presentation. For a couple of years, I only used a floating line and I caught plenty of pike.

Leaders

The leader is the length of clear line between the fly-line and the fly. It has to fulfil several functions. First, it must help disguise our efforts – heavy fly-line is very visible; the leader is much less so. Then it must help the fly-line to turn over the fly and deliver it as smoothly as possible. It must also be strong enough to stand up to the pounding it will take from a heavyweight, hard-fighting adversary. We need to achieve a sensible compromise between unobtrusiveness, performance and strength.

When I started fly-fishing for pike, I used simple, level monofilament. It had good knot strength, was reliable and easy to obtain. I later switched to fluorocarbon. Because this material has a similar refractive index to water, it is much less visible than monofilament. Since I found myself fishing for pike that were educated and wary, I wanted every possible advantage.

Another point I had learned from my trout fishing experience was that a tapered leader helped with turnover and presentation, so now, if I want optimum performance, I make a stepped-down leader. Typically, this will be made up of three sections. The butt is 33 lb monofilament, nail-knotted to my fly-line. The mid-section is 26 lb monofilament. The tippet is 18 lb fluoro-carbon. The three lengths each start out at 3 ft long. By the time they have been joined together, with four-turn water knots, I'm left with a leader of 7 ft 6 in. One can also buy ready-made, knotless tapered leaders. These are more convenient but do cost rather more. Also, as I sometimes want to make adjustments to my leader length, the homemade option can be more practical. The step-down or taper helps transfer casting energy from the fly-line to the leader, which means that the fly will be turned over more efficiently. If I'm not striving for casting performance, I'll often simply use 7 ft 6 in of 26 lb fluoro-carbon. A longer leader is stealthier – a shorter leader makes casting easier. If I'm faced with having to make a choice between the two, I'll usually opt for the shorter version. I can't catch a pike I can't cover and it can be a stealthier option to position the boat further from the taking zone. If I'm using a clear, intermediate line, I'll happily use a leader of 5 ft and if I'm fishing a buoyant fly on a high-density, sinking line, I may reduce my leader to 3 ft.

Traces

I attach a 1 ft wire trace to the end of my leader. Some anglers advocate the use of heavy-duty, hard nylon as a bite-guard trace – I don't. I have used hard nylon to tie weed-guards on pike flies, but I no longer bother as the pike bite through it. I don't want to leave a hook – even a barbless one – in a pike. I also hate losing good fish so I always use a wire trace.

There are various trace materials to choose from. I'll start by describing my current favourite option. This product goes by the name of American Fishing Wire. It has 49 strands and meets all of my requirements. It knots easily, is supple enough to resist kinking, it's fine compared to its breaking strain (26 lb) and is drab enough to be relatively unobtrusive. Perfect!

I realise that in a perfect world, we would all use the perfect material at all times. However, I can't always get it so do resort to other wires that are stocked by local tackle shops. Of these alternatives, the sweetest to use is an incredibly soft, multifilament thread. It's extremely supple and knots easily and reliably.

When marketed for fly-fishers, it goes by the name of Armor Pro Leader. I have also found what seems to be an identical material on sale in my local coarse fishing emporium under the brand name Supra Tress. I use a four-turn water knot to attach it to my leader and a Rapala knot to join it to my fly. The latter forms a loop which allows the fly to articulate perfectly. I use the thinnest option I have found on sale which has a breaking strain of 26 lb. This material doesn't kink and withstands the rigours of fly-casting extremely well. It does have one drawback – it's relatively visible, especially in clear water on a sunny day. In truth, this often doesn't present a problem, although sometimes it does.

Sometimes, I'm fishing for educated pike in clear water and I want my wire trace to be as unobtrusive as possible. In such circumstances, if I've run out of American Fishing Wire, I'll use old-fashioned, seven-strand pike-wire. This is thin, drab and relatively inconspicuous. I crimp my fly onto one end and crimp a 'rig ring' to the other, to which I can tie my leader. Properly done, this produces a reliable bite-guard trace. I stress 'properly done', as I am aware of several anglers who have experienced problems with the crimp connections. Always use crimps that are of a size compatible with the diameter of the wire and buy a tool which lets you squeeze the crimp in three places. This material is cheap and effective but it does have a significant disadvantage. It's very prone to kinking, which significantly reduces its strength. It needs to be checked frequently during the fishing session. Often, landing a lively pike will reduce it to a nasty corkscrew which you must discard and replace immediately.

Whichever material you are using, you will also need a set of cutters that will snip the wire cleanly. I use a set marketed by Fox under the name Trace Blades.

Making up your own traces can be a fiddly business. I've been doing it for years so don't regard it as a problem. Some anglers prefer the convenience of a ready-made trace. These usually come with a snap-link for attaching the fly and a loop or swivel at the other end for the leader to be tied to. When I started fly-fishing for pike, I used snap-links, but found that those small enough to allow my fly to fish effectively didn't stand up to the rigours of fly-fishing and I lost a couple of decent pike when the snap-link failed. I regard reliability as a more important factor than convenience. In truth, the convenience factor has become less relevant as I don't actually change my fly that often. I've caught enough pike to be confident in my fly selection so don't regard it as too much effort to tie, or crimp on, a replacement. In fact, if I expect to change flies during a session, I'll often start with a longer (18 in) wire trace to allow for the fact that each change will waste an inch or two of wire.

Landing gear

Having cast our fly and hooked a pike, our next concern is how to land it. Often my 'landing device' is my left hand. If the pike is small, I can grip it behind the head and lift it out of the water. Larger fish can be 'chinned'. To do this, you slide one hand under the gill cover to the sharp end of the pike, get a firm grip, from below, on the jawbone and lift smoothly bringing your other hand into play to support the pike from underneath. I don't recommend this for the inexperienced. Get an old hand to show you how it's done and don't try it yourself until you are confident. Too often, I've watched anglers play a pike to a standstill because they are worried about landing the fish by hand. This is bad practice and causes the pike unnecessary stress. If you are worried, use a net.

Sometimes, landing a pike by hand simply isn't a practical proposition. I have a big gye net (one where the handle slides up into the frame) made for salmon fishing by McLeans of New Zealand. Because the handle slides up into the frame, it can be stowed neatly in the bottom of a boat. It has a quick-release sling which makes it comfortable to carry on my back when bank fishing. In addition, there is a spring balance in the handle which means that I can weigh a big pike without any fuss. It's lightweight and robust – far stronger than the triangular framed nets with folding arms used by most coarse anglers. Most of my guiding clients have ended up buying the same model – I assure you I don't receive any sales commission!

Guiding clients are often amused by the size of my net. They have a different attitude after a big fish has been landed! It handles 20 lb pike easily. However, those around 30 lb are a bit of a squeeze. (I haven't caught a 40 lb pike yet. When I do, if it doesn't fit in the net, I'll get into the water and lift it out bodily!)

If I'm boat-fishing, there is always an unhooking mat in the bottom of the boat. I'll also take one if I'm bank fishing somewhere that doesn't have a suitably soft surface for unhooking a pike.

Unhooking gear

Having landed a pike, we now need to unhook it. This often makes the novice nervous. Again, don't go pike fishing on your own until you are comfortable with your ability to handle your catch. Many years ago, like most other pike anglers of the day, I employed a device called a gag (the Americans call this a jaw-spreader) to keep the pike's mouth open. This device was more like a medieval instrument of torture than a piece of fishing tackle. Of course now, like all serious modern pike fishers, I have learned how to hold a pike properly for unhooking. Further explanation of these matters is given in Chapter 16 Pressure, Care and Conservation. Again, I think this is a skill best learned in the company of an experienced, competent pike fisherman. Pike deserve our respect and are too valuable a fish to be stressed by a nervous, inexperienced angler taking too long to unhook them.

I carry a heavy-duty set of long-nosed pliers with bent jaws to extract my hook. I prefer these to less rigid artery forceps – which will, however, do an acceptable job. A trout fisher's smaller disgorger just isn't the tool for the task. Whilst I occasionally get grazed by the pike's teeth, I do still have a full set of fingers!

◄ When you have caught your pike, you need to be able to unhook it whilst retaining a full complement of fingers. My set of long-nosed pliers is the ideal tool for the job.
(Paul Armishaw)

Sundries

The flies I take for a pike-fishing session are housed in a deep, waterproof box marketed for accommodating tarpon flies. Some anglers favour a special type of wallet with clear plastic pockets. Personally, I prefer the way a rigid box protects my relatively bulky flies. My box holds a dozen flies. Which dozen is dependent on how I have assessed the conditions on the day. It fits in my tackle

► My deep fly-box
protects my 3d streamers
and can hold enough flies
for a fishing session.
(Andy Bowman)

bag, my wading jacket or the cartridge pocket of an old shooting waistcoat. If
I'm away on a pike-fishing expedition for a week, the boot of my Land Rover
will contain a larger compartmentalised box (sold to take plugs and spinners)
with a reserve of flies for the trip.

I regard good Polaroid sunglasses as an essential part of my fishing equipment. My tackle bag contains two pairs – one with brown lenses for sunny days
and one with yellow lenses for low light conditions. They serve two important
functions. First, they afford my eyeballs protection against 4/0 hooks travelling
at high velocity. Never take chances with this. Even the best casters can drop
the line and lose control of their cast. Also, you may find yourself with a boat
partner who has a cavalier attitude to his companion's health and safety. I
always insist that a guiding client wears eye protection at all times – no exceptions. Safety aside, good Polaroid lenses also let me see into the water better.
This can have a significant bearing on the success of my fishing efforts. If I spot
a pike following my fly, I have a far better chance of persuading it to take than if
I hadn't seen it. I'm also much less likely to spook a fish by splatting my fly-line
on its head. My fishing shades live in my tackle bag when I'm not using them.
They are kept purely for fishing. This avoids them being left on the dashboard
of my car or in the pocket of a jacket in my wardrobe.

I regard a hat as part of my fishing tackle rather than as an item of apparel
or a fashion accessory. A hat protects my head from misdirected ironmongery
and shields my eyes from the sun. I favour a wide-brimmed hat whenever
practical but will opt for a cap if it's blowing a gale.

◄ A hat, polarised glasses, a lifejacket and a waterproof, breathable wading jacket, keep me safe and comfortable. *(Andy Bowman)*

My tackle bag also contains a diamond hook hone. Pike have hard, bony mouths which can soon blunt a hook. I once spent a very frustrating couple of hours getting solid takes from pike that were feeding with enthusiasm. When I realised that it was my hook point that was the problem, I changed my fly and quickly landed a few fish. Ever since, I have made sure that I can sharpen a dull hook.

An old, Fahrenheit thermometer accompanies me on every pike-fishing trip. I log the temperature of the water, as keeping a record helps me to understand the rhythms of each venue that I fish. Accumulating data can give you invaluable information and help put more pike on the bank.

Because pike fishing is often done from a boat, it can be useful to have your own life-jacket. The ones aimed at fly-fishers are altogether neater than the ones which boat hirers usually supply. They don't restrict your casting and are very light to wear.

I used to have two sets of waders – heavy neoprene for cold conditions and ones made from breathable Gore-Tex for warmer days. My neoprene set has been consigned to the rubbish collection, having developed too many leaks to be worth repairing again. Also, they were fine when I was up to my armpits in cold water, but otherwise it was like walking around in my own, portable Turkish bath. This might have been useful if I had needed to lose weight, but it

▲ This favourite Irish lough is bordered by lillies and reeds. There isn't a convenient jetty so chest waders are essential for launching your boat.
(Andy Bowman)

could be desperately uncomfortable. By contrast, breathable chest waders let the perspiration out and are comfortable to wear but don't offer any thermal insulation. I overcome this with layers of breathable fleece undergarments which keep me as warm as I need to be. When I fish remote loughs in Ireland, I'm often faced with launching boats without any convenient jetty available. Sometimes, chest waders are the only sensible option. They can also allow me to work my way around marginal reed-beds when I'm fishing from the shore.

Sometimes, if I'm engaged in jungle warfare, fishing from overgrown banks, where the vegetation conspires to grab my fly-line, I'll use a line-tray. My first stripping basket was a homemade example, fashioned from an old washing-up bowl and a wading belt. I later progressed to a proprietary option that resembled a neoprene ice-cream bucket. The version I use now is marketed under the name Flexi-stripper. It is made up of a plastic tray with upright nylon prongs, which store the fly-line in coils which don't (normally!) tangle. Like most fly-fishers, I find a line tray a nuisance to lug around but reckon that there are some circumstances that demand its use.

This chapter contains a comprehensive list of the equipment I have available for my pike fly-fishing – although I have omitted other specialist items such as motors, anchors, belly-boats and echo-sounders. However, don't get the wrong idea. I don't lug everything around with me all the time. One of the special pleasures of fly-fishing is that you can travel light. Often, a rod, a reel, some leader material, a couple of flies and my long-nosed pliers are all that accompany me.

Chapter 3

FLIES FOR PIKE

Tʜᴇ sᴀᴠᴀɢᴇ, ᴠᴏʀᴀᴄɪᴏᴜs ᴘɪᴋᴇ is reputed to devour any and every living creature in the water. Fish, including other pike, rodents, wildfowl, un-wary Jack Russell terriers and (if old wives' tales are to be believed) even maid-servants from large country houses have all fallen victim to the pike's ferocity.

I've seen a pike take ducklings from the surface and I've caught a large pike with a coot down its throat. Whilst I'm sure that an opportunistic pike will grab a meal where it can, I'm also sure that fish make up the bulk of any large pike's diet. Because of this, I tie my flies to imitate, or at least suggest, prey-fish.

The first requirement I have of a pike-fly is that it should look as if it's worth eating. A 20 lb pike is more likely to burn calories catching something sub-stantial than pursuing a 3 in fry. With this in mind, my standard flies are tied large – 6 to 7 in long – and sometimes I will use flies that are larger still. I also tie most of my flies to be three-dimensional, so that they look appealing when viewed from below. This is important, as it's often how a pike will view the fly.

There are occasional exceptions to the 'bigger is better' principle. My guiding client, Sean Bobbitt, has caught pike on small deceivers when they have been hammering massed fry – pike that I'd failed to catch on larger flies. However these exceptions are occasional. Pike rarely become preoccupied with fry in the way that trout can.

In his classic book, *The Pursuit of Stillwater Trout*, Brian Clarke questions what motivates a trout to take a fly. He offers three possible explanations – curiosity, aggression and hunger. He opts for using patterns which imitate the trout's natural food as the approach to ensure consistently successful fishing. Overall, I have come to the same conclusion with my pike fishing. I say 'overall' because pike are not trout and we have additional factors to consider which don't apply to fishing for trout.

A trout needs to eat a large number of small creatures to thrive. A pike needs to grow to survive. As a small fish, it is both predator and prey. Only when it has grown to a good size is it safe from the gastronomic attentions of its larger relatives. On the morning that I caught my first 30 lb pike, I had an 11 lb fish grabbed by a huge pike as I was trying to land it. Since pike get their nourishment from larger prey than do trout this means that they tend to feed less often and for shorter periods. Often, we have to persuade the pike to hit our lovingly crafted imitation roach pattern in preference to hundreds of samples of the real thing. We can attempt to make our fly attractive by making it look like a substantial mouthful. We can also make it appealing by imparting an action which makes it look like an easy meal – a vulnerable victim, worth singling-out for attack.

Sometimes, we are faced with pike that have filled their bellies and show no interest in chasing our flies. Then, sometimes, we can trigger a reaction by provoking not a 'hungry' response but an 'aggressive' one.

On 16 June 2006, the opening day of the season, I was fishing my local old estate lake. I had made some visits to check out the water over the preceding days and I knew where some good pike were in residence. I fished my way along a stretch of bank, carefully working my sub-surface streamer close to the emerging weed-beds and the marginal reeds. An hour and a half later, I was feeling frustrated, my easy confidence seemed to have been misplaced. I cut the streamer off my wire trace and crimped on a red and white, plastazote headed, surface popper. I then started to work my way back along the same stretch of bank. I cast my fly, which landed on the mirror-calm surface of the lake with a resounding 'splat' that sent ripples over the water. I slowly tightened my floating line to the fly, causing as little disturbance as possible. Then I gave my line a sharp tug with my left hand. The popper kicked and spluttered, setting up a fair commotion. I was about to start a slow, erratic retrieve, when the water beneath the fly erupted. A yard of green and gold launched itself out of the water with my fly in its jaws. I took three more good pike on my way back – pike that had been disinterested in my previous offers.

My pike-flies have to fulfil a number of objectives. They must look good, convincing the pike that they are a tasty meal rather than just an object in the water. They must behave in an attractive, enticing way that reinforces their visual appearance. They must work, in partnership with particular fly-lines and leaders, to allow me to present my fly at the right depth and the right speed. They must be durable – a pike's impressive array of teeth can reduce a fly, tied from delicate materials, to a soggy, shredded mess. In the next few pages I'll describe the patterns I use to catch pike consistently throughout the year. I'll also explain how to fish the various flies, what tackle to combine them with and in what circumstances to use them. In the following chapter I'll describe the dressings so that any fly-tiers reading this book will be able to reproduce the patterns and I have included a step by step, illustrated sequence, showing how to construct my most frequently used fly. I have, however, avoided turning these chapters into a lengthy manual on fly-tying – it would make dull reading for anyone who just wants to buy pike-flies from a tackle shop or prefers to commission a fly-tier to make some. At the time of writing this, I am also in the process of producing a separate book of pike-fly patterns with detailed, illustrated tying instructions that will enable the raw beginner to produce first-rate flies.

The basic 3d streamer

This fly was once christened Dodds' 3d Dodger by Mark Bowler, the illustrious editor of *Fly-Fishing and Fly-tying* magazine. In the course of every year, it accounts for around 90 per cent of the pike that I catch. The synthetic winging materials shed water, which makes it relatively easy to cast. The materials used and the construction of the fly make it robustly durable. My fly-box will often contain examples that have led to the capture of more than twenty pike and are still serviceable. It incorporates an epoxy head which gives it a weight-forward action. It sinks slowly, in a gentle, nose-first way and can be tweaked up in the water, very enticingly, when fished on a floating line. This fly is tied to give a good, solid, three-dimensional, profile. This means that it looks worth chasing when viewed from below, which is crucial to its success. A pike's eyes are set to give good, forward, binocular vision, a typical predator characteristic. They are also set high on the pike's head, enabling it to use weed growth for cover and to focus on the prey-fish swimming above. Pike will often hit this fly high in the water, giving us exciting visual takes. It has enough movement to look alive in the water without having a crazy, exaggerated wriggle to destroy the illusion.

In May 2007, I was fishing Llangorse Lake in South Wales with a guiding client. We took a boat out with the early morning mist shrouding the water and not a breath of wind to ruffle the surface. The watery, early sun put in an

► My basic 3d streamer is tied to suggest a prey-fish. This example makes a good representation of a perch. The fly sinks slowly. The weight of the head, formed with Kevlar thread and epoxy, allows me to impart an enticing, jigging action to the fly.

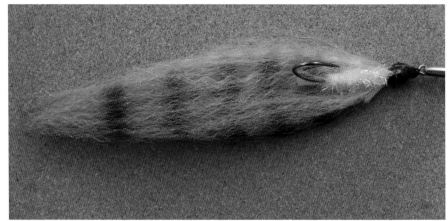

► The same 3d streamer when viewed from below has a substantial profile. The pike certainly think it's worth burning calories to chase it!

appearance and started to burn off the haze. We found some pike. They were hammering a huge shoal of perch, just off the newly emerging lilies. The pike were swirling dramatically, scattering small perch as they attacked. The fishing method was simple. We cast at a swirl, let the imitative, perch-pattern streamer sink for a few seconds, then started to slowly tweak the fly back. The sport was furious. Every cast produced a sharp hit (we didn't connect with a pike every time) and we brought nine pike, including a couple of good fish, to the boat in the first hour. The next hour produced eight pike and the third hour six battling fish. The sun climbed in the clear blue sky and the pike switched off. We didn't care!

The pike had picked our perch-pattern flies out of thousands of small perch that had been driven to the surface. Because our flies had appeared out of synch with the rest of the shoal, they had been singled out for attack. Two very satisfied fly-fishers docked the boat at the jetty and enjoyed a good shore lunch.

We had been lucky. The conditions had been perfect. Clear, quite shallow water and pike feeding actively in a defined area made it an ideal day. In such fortunate circumstances, a 3d streamer, tied to imitate the prey-fish and fished with a floating line, provides the perfect method.

We're not always so fortunate. Sometimes, the water will be coloured by sediment, washed into the lake by flooded feeder streams. In such circumstances, I'll opt to use a more visible version of the same fly. I've found yellow and orange to be a particularly effective solution when fishing coloured water. Strangely, these hi-viz flies seem to work much less well when the water is clear. The pike notice them and will often follow the fly but refuse to take it.

I generally use a floating line when fishing the 3d streamer. If it's blowing a gale, I may opt for a sink-tip line to avoid the problem of having my fly skated across the surface by the waves. If I want to fish the fly low in the water, in deeper water, I may use a slow-sinking intermediate line. This can be a particularly effective method of fishing 'down the slope' when casting at the margins from a boat anchored beyond the drop-off.

I tie the 3d streamer in a variety of colours – various prey-fish imitations, hi-viz and 'provocative' combinations. The photographs illustrate the range that's possible. Obtaining varnish to finish the epoxy heads has become a pleasure in itself. I use ladies' nail varnish: the lovely barmaid in my village pub

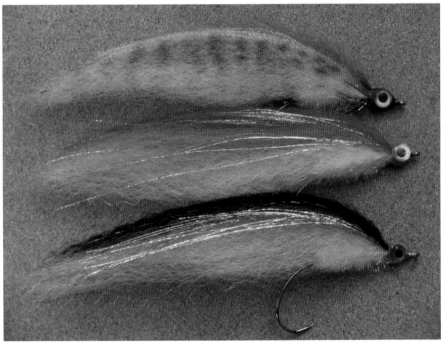

◄ A selection of 3d streamers. These have been tied to suggest prey-fish and will be my first choices when the water is reasonably clear. Which particular fly I will use will be determined by the pikes' predominant prey.

supplies me with her cast-offs. I have a dazzling range of colours and a perfect excuse to go for a pint and engage beautiful young ladies in conversation. My son, now a strapping, athletic teenager, has also found it to be a disarming and highly original chat-up line!

► This yellow and orange streamer is my favourite option for fishing when there is colour in the water. Then, it can prove extremely effective but it is markedly less successful in clear water conditions.

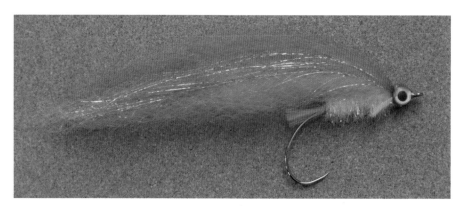

The popper

This fly should carry a Government Health Warning! The spectacular surface takes that it produces give the fly-fisherman the most fun to be had in fresh-water. The excitement level is too extreme for anyone with a heart condition.

I was prompted to experiment with poppers after a June evening spent fishing with my son, then 8 years old, on our local old estate lake. I was fly-fishing and Sebastian was flipping out a floating plug. We were both enjoying some good sport as the light faded and the surface of the lake became mirror-calm, as often happens in the evening. Sebastian switched to using a saltwater 'Skitterpop'. He had fun. Pike erupted from underneath his popper, spraying water in all directions. He caught a few more pike and lost a very big fish, which shed the hook after tail-walking and stripping line from his reel in a screaming, unstoppable run.

I was impressed. I wanted some of this exhilarating, top of the water sport for myself – it was too good for boys! Later that evening, I sat behind my vice, determined to create a fly that would produce the same effect as my son's lure. I fashioned a head from a wine bottle cork and, the next morning, I returned to the lake at first light. Full of tingling anticipation, I made my way to the same bay we had fished the previous evening. The new fly worked. The second cast produced an explosion of white water as a pike leapt with my fly in its jaws. After a stunning, acrobatic fight, I landed a beautiful double-figure pike. Sadly,

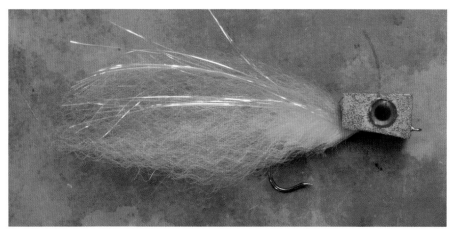

◀ A simple, dished plastazote head gives the popper its buoyancy and helps it to kick up a fuss when it's retrieved. The head is set high on the hook shank to keep the gape clear for the best hooking performance. Pike take this fly in an explosion of white water, which puts the pulse-rate into overdrive!

it was the only pike that my experimental fly produced. The pike's impressive set of teeth had completely shredded the cork head.

Realising that I needed a better material, I started to investigate. I settled on plastazote – Veniard sell it in neat blocks in a useful range of colours. I chose this material, a fairly dense, rather soft foam, despite it being more difficult to shape than hard foam. Because it is compressible, it seems to give a higher proportion of hooked fish and any damage to a varnished finish is simple enough to touch up. It provides the buoyancy that I want and stands up reasonably well to the ravages of the pikes' teeth. I use a model maker's scalpel to shape the head and dish the front to emphasise the 'popping' effect.

Pike view poppers from below and it's this silhouette view which needs to convince them that the fly is worth hitting. I give my poppers some bulk by tying an under-body (usually UV Fritz) on the hook shank. I wind this over a base of Kevlar thread, liberally coated with tacky white nail varnish. Using the varnish to glue the construction together prevents the fly from unravelling if the Fritz is cut by the pikes' teeth. I leave enough space behind the eye of the hook to allow me to fit the head, and I notch the head at the back so that it fits over the winging material, without leaving a 'hole' in the fly.

My tackle set-up for fishing the popper is simple. I attach the fly to a 12 in wire trace, which is joined to an 8 ft fluorocarbon leader of around 25 lb breaking strain. I use Varivas, Seaguar or Rio. These all knot reliably and have never let me down. I degrease the leader with Richard Walker's Leadersink. This, combined with the fact that fluorocarbon is denser than standard monofilament line, means that my leader cuts through the surface tension and doesn't leave a tell-tale bulge along the top of the water. This is particularly important in the mirror-calm conditions that I often choose to fish poppers in.

I most often use poppers in the late spring for post-spawn pike that are still holding in the shallow, weedy bays where they spawned earlier in the year. Frequently, I'll be fishing from the bank but sometimes I'll don my breathable chest waders or take to a boat, if it's necessary in order to cover the right piece of water. I'll be as stealthy in my approach as possible, utilising any available cover and keeping a low profile. Flat-calm conditions most often occur at first light and at dusk (usually the best times to fish at this time of year). A set of light-enhancing, yellow lens, polarised glasses are a valuable addition to my equipment.

I'll resist the urge to just cast and fish, first studying the water in front of me with care. Sometimes, a pike can be spotted lying motionless, close to the surface. Even then, I'll fight the temptation to cast. There could be another fish between me and my quarry, which would be spooked by casting over it and could well alarm every pike in the bay. There could also be a pike, tight in the margins, which would be startled by me waving a fly-rod over its head. If I'm fortunate enough to have a pike in my sights, I'll cast in front and beyond it. I'll let the popper sit on the surface and I'll tighten my fly-line to it, causing as little disturbance as possible. I'll then look to cause some disturbance, giving my line a definite jerk of a foot or so. On the right day, the pike will accelerate straight onto the fly and the fun will start!

More often, the pike will be harder to spot. Then it's best to cover the water methodically, by casting in a fan. I do this twice, first with short casts to avoid 'lining' fish close to me, then I'll repeat the process with longer casts. Having created my initial, attention-grabbing disturbance, I'll retrieve the fly slowly and erratically, making it twitch, splutter and pause, trying to make it look like the pike's favourite meal – a fish in distress. I fish every cast right to my toes. I've lost count of the number of times that I've had a pike hit my fly right at the end of my retrieve, just prior to lifting-off to recast. This is where the importance of good, polarised glasses is most evident. If you see a pike coming for your fly, you can try to persuade it to take. If you don't see it, you can drag your fly off the water, advertise your presence to the pike and spook it. Having a 20 lb pike hit your fly right under your nose is too good an experience to miss. You'll find out whether your rod is up to the job of fishing for pike. I've had a few break under the sudden, extreme stress of dealing with an angry pike on a short line. However, the right rod won't let you down and will cope well, even if your pulse rate is sent into overdrive.

In my experience, some waters respond much better to popper fishing than others. I've had guiding clients and have met other, perfectly good fly-fishers, who have struggled to catch pike on poppers. It's hard to be scientific about it but my gut feeling is that waters with a good wildfowl population give the best chance of some action. I used to regard popper fishing as an entertaining method rather than a mainstream, fish-catching tactic, but the last few seasons have changed my opinion. There have been plenty of occasions when the popper has been the most successful option. For me, it's been a technique that has worked best during a specific time of the year – mid-May until mid-July – and in specific conditions – mirror-calm, windless days. Mark Corps, a splendid pike fly-fisher and fellow guide based in Ireland, has experienced different results. He took out a client in November 2007 and the fishing was slow and hard. Mark's client insisted on trying a popper. Mark explained that the popper only worked in warmer weather. The client proceeded to catch eleven pike on his popper, whilst Mark continued to struggle. Like I've said before, none of us can hope to solve all the mysteries of fly-fishing for pike!

Catching pike on a popper is too exciting an experience to miss out on. The sight of a huge bow wave accelerating behind your fly or the sudden, unexpected explosion from beneath the water is an experience to savour. Enjoy it and repeat it as often as possible!

The bomber

The previous two flies described work superbly well when the pike are 'on' and the conditions are good, but we're not always so lucky. Sometimes, we're faced with pike that are glued to the bottom in deeper water and disinclined to come up and chase a fly. For me, the bomber is a method of last resort, for the dog-days of summer and for sudden cold snaps in the dark depths of winter.

I 'stole' the technique from Alan Hanna, who describes it in his book *Fly Fishing for Big Pike*. He uses it as his first-choice method. My opinion is different; it's not my 'prime-time' fly. Sure – it can catch pre-spawn, post-spawn and on those magical days in the autumn. However, other flies and other methods are better able to exploit the opportunities offered at these special times.

Essentially, the bomber is like the trout angler's 'booby' – a buoyant fly, fished on a sinking line. The mechanical principles are the same but my style of fishing the fly is different.

I attach my bomber to a 1 ft wire trace and a short, 3 ft leader. I join this to a high-density (sink rate of 8 in per second) shooting head. (I've described the principles and construction of shooting heads in the previous chapter.) After casting, I allow the weight of the shooting head to sink the fly. With the

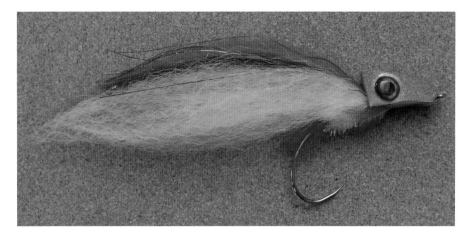

▶ The bomber – a
buoyant fly to fish on a
fast-sinking shooting head.
It's a fly which will tempt
pike when they are dour
and inactive.

high-density head on the bottom of the lake, the buoyant bomber will be tethered above. A retrieve will make the fly dive. A pause will allow it to flutter upwards enticingly. My retrieve is a slow, erratic combination of pulls, pauses and tweaks. As always, I'm trying to make my fly look like an easy meal – particularly important when fishing for dour pike. Takes often come immediately after a pause, so always be prepared when you tweak the fly. (The word 'often' refers to overall ratio, as you won't get that many takes in a single session!)

Because you're not in 'straight line' contact with your fly, takes need to be hit very firmly. Merely giving your rod a casual waft won't do the trick. I use the tarpon fisher's 'strip-strike' technique, pulling the running line sharply with my left hand, at the same time as I bend the rod with my right hand. The cushion effect of a good fly-rod means that you can put more 'grunt' into this than you might expect. Sometimes, takes are felt as a good, firm pull, at other times, the line just 'gets heavy'. In any case, when you're connected to a pike, it's important to get your drowned line up in the water so that you can maintain straight-line contact with the pike and keep your hook-hold.

Essentially, this is a method for deeper (over 10 ft) stillwaters. It works from the bank, whilst wading, or from a boat. When boat-fishing, I prefer to fish with the boat anchored at both ends for maximum stability. As always, stealth is important. I'll make my final approach to the deep, holding spot, either by drifting or by using the oars.

Because this fly is fished down to where the pike are lurking, there is less need for it to have a pronounced, three-dimensional profile – so important when a fly is fished high in the water. It will be viewed more 'side on' so it is this, two-dimensional, shape which needs to stimulate the pike. This means that we can make a big fly thinner (relatively!) and easier to cast long distances.

I generally tie my bombers to be somewhat larger than Al Hanna's Bally-doolagh Bomber. I also use different materials, preferring modern synthetics, which are more durable than the bucktail of the original. As with the popper, the head is made from plastazote and is finished with nail varnish. The head is shaped to be rather more streamlined than the popper and its size is crucial. It needs to be large enough to be buoyant in itself but not so large that the weight of the shooting head won't sink it to allow it to be fished in the bottom few feet of the lake.

Bumping a fly along the bottom isn't my favourite way to fly-fish. It's slow, painstaking and lacks the visual excitement of other methods. Shooting heads are less pleasant to cast than full fly-lines. On some days however, we're faced with a stark choice, to fish with a method that at least gives us the chance of a pike, or to stay in a comfortable bed and wait for warmer weather! Whilst it isn't my favourite method, it must be said that it does produce some sizeable pike. When you're fishing the special deeper water in the depths of winter, there's every chance that the prime spot will be home to the biggest, most dominant, old-lady pike. Because it's a method that I only resort to when the conditions are hard and the pike are dour, I can't claim that I have taken great hauls of fish on it. I have, though, landed some spectacular pike on the bomber and regard it as a useful technique.

The double bunny

This is a fly to keep in reserve for when you need an edge. It has more movement, more wriggle than a basic 3d streamer tied with synthetic materials. On occasions, this extra mobility will get a reaction from a pike that isn't really 'in the mood'. The natural materials – rabbit fur strip and, sometimes, a wing collar made from marabou 'bloods' or schlappen feathers – can be used to produce aesthetically pleasing flies. Most fly-tiers derive a special pleasure from making pretty flies.

These flies do come with some significant disadvantages. They soak up water, which makes them more of a problem to cast. The materials are also more susceptible to damage from the pike's impressive armoury of teeth. That said, these flies catch plenty of pike and my fly-box always contains a few examples.

In the past, I stuck the two tails together with Aquaseal, a waterproof glue used for repairing waders. I reasoned that this would make my fly look more natural. However, I no longer do this. I have found that the separate tails retain more enticing wriggle and work together perfectly well. I tie in a loop at the end

► The double bunny can be tied in a wide range of colours to be imitative, provocative or hi-viz. The highly mobile rabbit fur strips impart an exagge-rated wriggle, which, on some days, can trigger a response from a reluctant pike.

of the hook shank to project above and beyond the bend. This helps to prevent the rabbit fur strips tangling around the bend of the hook whilst casting. I say 'helps' advisedly because it isn't a perfect solution and there will still be occasions when you have to tidy-up the fly prior to recasting.

During the three prime times for pike fishing – pre-spawn, post-spawn and the autumn 'stocking-up' period – I'll normally stick with conventional 3d streamers. Why should I give myself problems when I don't have to? I'm most likely to opt for a double bunny when the pike are less active. 'Less active' doesn't mean uncatchable, and a cold day in January will often see me working a double bunny along a drop-off, searching for a pike that wants a tasty snack.

I'm more likely to tie this fly on a 6/0 hook than a 4/0. If I'm feeling par-ticularly macho, I'll go as large as 8/0. Because of the bulkiness of these flies, I'll use my 10 weight rod more often than my 9 weight. Because I'm most likely to use these large 'winter tempter' flies when it's cold, I won't expect a fish every cast but often the pike hooked in these circumstances will be sizeable. Big pike seem to be less deterred by cold conditions than their smaller brethren. I'll make a point of taking a break during the session to drink strong coffee, warm my hands and perhaps fill my pipe with strong baccy. It's not good to fish to the point where you get mechanical and lose concentration. That elusive take, when it comes, could be from a pike that will more than compensate for the pains of slow fishing in finger-numbing, cold conditions.

The rattler

This is essentially a variation of the double bunny – a variation that adds noise into the package. Like the double bunny, it's a fly for quite specific circum-stances. It proved particularly useful in 2007. At the start of the year, winter floods had turned my local old estate lake into something resembling cold cocoa. There was some respite from these difficult, coloured water conditions during the spring, but July brought unseasonable, torrential rain. The local rivers covered the fields, and the lake was positively opaque. The rattler had caught me some pike during the previous winter so, whilst I wasn't bursting with confidence, I knew that there was still the chance of a pike, provided that I was fishing in the right location.

▲ The rattler adds noise to the process. It gets noticed even in conditions that many would dismiss as being unsuitable for fly-fishing. It has caught me several spectacular pike in water that was almost opaque. Sadly, it isn't the 'magic fly' – rather a 'last resort' that will produce a good fish in spite of poor conditions. Because I normally use the fly in heavily coloured water, I tend to tie it in hi-viz patterns.

The rattler gets noticed. A pike's sensory systems are highly developed. Not only is a pike's binocular vision more effective under water than we would imagine, its neuromast system detects noise and vibration over a considerable distance. This system comprises receptors along the lateral line of the fish and around the jaw which enable it to locate a potential meal. The pike is a predator of great efficiency – a predator that has developed to be successful and to thrive. If pike relied solely on vision to catch their prey, they would struggle to survive in England with our unpredictable weather.

To produce the rattler I tie a rattle, consisting of a small tube containing three tiny ball-bearings, below the under-body on the hook shank. Rattling, 'goggle eyes', complete the pattern. I generally use hi-viz colours for the dressing. The result isn't the most convincing imitative pattern but it does get noticed!

My first-ever outing with a rattler produced an interesting result. I was fishing the hatch-pool on the feeder stream that flows into my local estate lake. It was autumn and, as in previous years, some large pike had pinned a huge number of small prey-fish in the fish-trap. There had been heavy rainfall over the preceding few days and the water was turbulent, with the opacity of cold, milky tea. I had a take on my first cast – at least I thought I had; there was so much debris bobbing around in the water that it was hard to be certain. I made another cast into the slack water by an eddy. This time, there was no un-certainty. My right shoulder was nearly dislocated by a really savage take and the fight was on. I couldn't let the pike run, as there were sunken trees close by, so had to hold on and keep applying side-strain to turn the fish. After an exciting few minutes, I was relieved to get her over the net – a superb pike of more than 24 lb. I was elated. I was convinced that I'd found the ultimate solution to catching pike from coloured water. A couple of hours later, my conviction started to dissipate. The following morning produced a similar result – one decent fish (not a twenty) then nothing.

I've since come to the conclusion that the rattler is a useful rather than a magical fly. It has helped me to catch the odd, often sizeable, pike in conditions that conventional wisdom would have dismissed as hopeless for fly-fishing, but it hasn't caught me a great haul of pike in any conditions. Thinking that what worked in poor conditions might prove irresistible in good conditions, I tried the rattler in good clear water. It provoked a reaction, pike followed it, they tailed it but they didn't hit it. Often, when I fish with a guiding client, I'll use a different method from that which I advise my client to use. It's a useful control to ensure that we select the most effective technique for the day. In good water conditions, a 3d streamer has always out-fished the rattler.

The large tandem

Until recently, I wouldn't have included this pattern in the book. I had used seriously large flies and had caught pike with them. What I hadn't done, was catch a good pike with them when all else had failed. I had used flies a foot long sometimes just to show my fishing companion that it could be done. Sometimes, there had almost been a competitive element to it – who could cast the bigger fly! An experience in March 2008 changed my opinion. I was guiding with Mike Duxbury, an accomplished pike fly-fisher. We were struggling. Mike had booked three days to fish for pre-spawn pike but the fish were running behind schedule. We found ourselves fishing for stubbornly dour winter pike. The first day had produced a take from a solitary small jack, which had shed the hook. Day two had seen one double-figure pike slowly follow and ignore my fly. We were fishing at anchor in a sheltered bay that was deeper than the bays we knew the pike would come to spawn in. Mike had a sizeable pike take his streamer, kite lethargically across in front of me and drop the fly. It was frustrating. We stopped fishing and I poured strong coffee to revive our spirits as we discussed tactics. We had covered every cubic inch of the bay with our 7 in, 3d streamers. We knew that at least one big girl was in residence but had failed to get a confident take.

Mike decided that a drastic situation called for a drastic response. He removed his fly and produced something from the depths of his tackle bag that resembled a white chicken. It was a foot long creation of EP fibres shot through with UV sparkle mounted on a tandem rig of two 4/0 hooks. Some hot orange

◄ Mike Duxbury's foot long tandem. Not for the faint-hearted or the inexpert caster. It makes a convincing suggestion of 1 lb prey-fish and can catch the pike that can't be bothered to move for a snack but wants a one-hit feed.

fibres had been incorporated to suggest fins. He wound in his line and swapped his spool for one holding a special, short, floating shooting head that would load his 10/11 weight rod. Mike is a very good caster (he needed to be!) and proceeded to launch his fly into the corner of the bay. In the water, the big tandem fly made a pretty convincing imitation of a 1 lb roach. It sank horizontally and oh so slowly. Mike retrieved the fly at snail's pace, drawing it up enticingly in the water.

'Oh yes!' Mike's exclamation said it all. His rod was pulled into a dramatic curve as the pike powered away. This was no half-hearted pluck but a good, arm-wrenching hit – the pike was on! A few minutes later, I had the net under a good 20 lb pike. She had completely engulfed the huge fly but the barbless hooks were removed quickly and Mike held her up for the photograph.

There is a 'chicken' in the bottom of my tackle bag now. I won't use it if the pike are being co-operative. There is a fair bit of wear and tear involved in casting such large flies all day. However, if I'm faced with a specimen pike that needs a particularly tasty offering, then I'll grit my teeth and get physical!

I realise that the small number of pike-fly patterns that I have described and recommended will disappoint some readers. Sure, I have caught pike on flies tied to suggest mice, rats, frogs and ducklings. Some of my fishing companions delight in using crazy creations. However, this book is intended to be a useful and practical guide to catching pike with a fly-rod. Because of that, I have limited the fly selection. It's often better to just have a small choice of flies, all of which you are confident in. Too many choices can generate confusion and uncertainty. By all means, if fly-tying is your passion, invent fantastical flies and catch pike with them!

Chapter 4

PATTERNS AND TYING INSTRUCTIONS

A POINT WORTH MAKING at the start of this chapter is that I always tie my own pike flies on barbless hooks. If I tie flies for customers, I always use barbless hooks. Sure, the odd pike comes adrift but pike come adrift when anglers use barbed hooks. The problem is whether the pike was properly hooked in the first place. Anyone who loses a pike by not playing it effectively should just lick his wounds and resolve to do better next time. Pike are a valuable game fish. They are all wild fish and don't get stocked into waters. It is vital that we protect this resource. Barbless, single hooks allow us to release pike in the shortest possible time and with the minimum of stress – that's the end of my sermon!

In this chapter, I will explain in detail how to tie the fly that I use to catch the majority of my pike every year. Learning how to produce this basic, three-dimensional streamer (christened Dodds' 3d dodger, by Mark Bowler, the editor of *Flyfishing & Flytying*) will equip you to tie all manner of variations that will allow you to solve practical fishing problems. For the other patterns in this chapter, I have simply included a picture and a list of tying materials. I have also illustrated any specific techniques that may not be obvious from the instructions. I feel that to include detailed tying instructions for each pattern would involve much repetition and would not interest most readers.

► The aim is to produce a fly that looks and behaves like a prey-fish. We are striving to persuade the pike that our offering is a plump, juicy fish rather than a bunch of material being dragged through the water. This fly does the job.

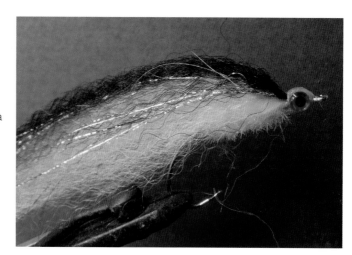

Dodds' 3d dodger

Dressing

Hook – Partridge, Ad Swier Absolute pike fly hook; size 4/0 or 6/0

Thread – Kevlar

Fins – H2O Fluorofibre (usually hot orange)

Under-body – Lureflash UV Fritz

Winging material – H2O Slinky Fibre and Flashabou (or similar)

Head – Epoxy, finished with nail varnish in an appropriate colour

Eyes – Lureflash 3d epoxy eyes

Adhering to these specific materials isn't compulsory! If you find others that give you a result that you prefer, that's fine. I don't regard fly 'recipes' as sacrosanct, rather as a useful guide that an individual can build on and modify.

1 Place the hook in the vice and check it for soundness. Starting at the eye of the hook, wind the Kevlar thread in close turns all the way down the shank to the bend.

2 Tie in the fins just before the bend. Do this by tying in on one side then 'double back' to produce the fin on the other side. Trim to size with scissors. 'Doubling back' means that the fibres are very secure and not at risk of being

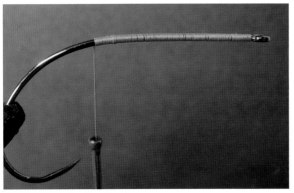

Step 1

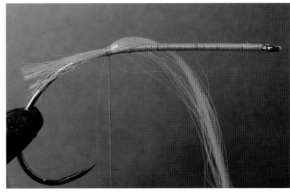

Step 2

Step 3

Step 4

pulled out by the pikes' teeth. Retain the off-cut of the Fluorofibre as this will be used for the pectoral fins later in the tying process.

3 Strip the fibres off the last few millimetres of the flue of the UV Fritz. Tie in the flue securely, adding a dollop of nail varnish to the tying. Wind the Kevlar thread back up the shank to the point where you will start to form the head. Dob some tacky old nail varnish along the Kevlar.

4 Wind the UV Fritz along the shank, over the bed of nail varnish. Tie in at the point where you will start to form the head (again, it's best to strip the fibres off the flue). By bedding the UV Fritz on the varnish, you avoid the problem of the under-body unravelling if the flue is bitten through by the pike's teeth.

5 Tie in white H2O Slinky Fibre on one side of the hook shank at the head. Trim off excess material. Do the same on the other side of the hook shank.
    Incorporate some nail varnish into the tying and use the strength of the Kevlar thread to tie tightly and make the fibres secure. By tying in the Slinky

Fibre on both sides of the hook, you achieve the three-dimensional effect which makes the fly look appealing when viewed from below.

6 Comb through. Cut the Slinky Fibre to shape with your fly-tying scissors. Then use hairdressers' thinning scissors to reduce the thickness of the fibres towards the tail of the fly. This is achieved by making the first thinning cut around the middle of the fly and making a further three or four, evenly spaced, cuts towards the tail of the fly. This thinning gives a beautifully tapered shape and helps impart lifelike mobility to the fly.

7 Take the retained off-cut bunch of Fluorofibre and tie it in at the middle, on one side of the hook shank, behind the head. Double back and tie in on the other side to produce the opposite pectoral fin. Again, by incorporating nail varnish into the tying, doubling back and cranking everything together with the Kevlar thread, you will be creating an extremely robust fly.

8 Tie in Slinky Fibre on top of the shank, behind the head and trim off excess material. Again, use the hairdressers' thinning scissors to taper the material

Step 5

Step 6

Step 7

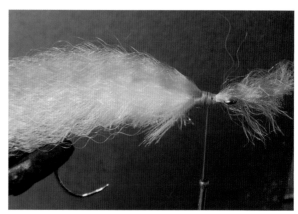
Step 8

towards the tail of the fly. It isn't necessary to tie in on the sides now as we already have a substantial profile when the fly is viewed from below. In the example shown, I'm tying in silver-grey material as I want to produce a fly that suggests a roach.

Step 9

9 Tie in the Flashabou and trim off the excess material. In the example shown, I'm using silver Flashabou to reinforce the appearance of a plump roach.

10 Tie in black Slinky Fibre on top of the fly to produce the back of the roach. Trim off the excess material and again, use the hairdressers' thinning scissors to taper the fibres. Continue to build extremely tight turns of Kevlar thread to form the shape of the head, incorporating nail varnish for total security. Whip finish.

Step 10

11 Mix the two-part epoxy on a clean card. Remove the fly from the vice and use a cocktail stick to apply the epoxy to the head. Use epoxy which sets in 10 minutes or less. Keep rotating the fly to prevent the epoxy from running. Fit the eyes. You can handle these carefully with your fingertips to help shape the head.

12 When the epoxy has set sufficiently to keep its shape, park the fly on a foam block and leave it so that the head can cure.

Step 11

13 Use nail varnish to finish the head.

14 Take the finished fly to your nearest old estate lake and catch a monster.

This basic pattern can be tweaked in many ways to produce a whole range of attractive patterns. You can use a variety of colours and blends of colours to suggest different prey-fish species.

Step 13

The Dodds' 3d dodger with additional feather tail

The example above has the addition of a feather tail which is attached to a length of classical guitar string (G 3rd). This one has deceived a fair few pike, including a 20 lb fish. At some point, the pikes' teeth will render the tail too tatty to be appealing – then, I'll simply snip off the guitar string to leave me with a basic 3d streamer. You can use pantone marker pens to add stripes for perch patterns or spots for trout or jack pike patterns.

The popper

Dressing

Hook – Partridge, Ad Swier Absolute pike fly hook; size 4/0 or 6/0

Thread – Kevlar

Fins – H2O Fluorofibre

Under-body – Lureflash UV Fritz

Winging material – H2O Slinky Fibre and Flashabou

Head – Plastazote

Eyes – Orvis Prismatic – the largest size

1 The winging material is tied in further back from the eye of the hook than when tying the 3d streamer.

The popper

2 As with the 3d streamer, the winging material is tied in on both sides of the hook shank, to give the fly a substantial profile when viewed from below.

3 Less material is needed for the top of the fly.

Steps 1, 2, 3

Step 4

4 The plastazote head is cut to shape with a scalpel. It is notched at the back to fit over the dressing. A slit is cut out of the bottom of the head so that it can be mounted on top of the fly. It is secured with epoxy. The front of the head is dished with a scalpel to produce the characteristic popping effect.

My early poppers had the hook shank through the middle of the head. I now mount the head higher on the hook to leave the hook gape as clear as possible. This has improved my hook-up rate.

The bomber

Dressing

Hook – Partridge, Ad Swier Absolute pike fly hook; size 4/0 or 6/0

Thread – Kevlar

Fins – H2O Fluorofibre

Under-body – Lureflash UV Fritz

Winging material – H2O Slinky Fibre and Flashabou

Head – Plastazote

Eyes – Orvis Prismatic (the largest size)

The bomber

1 As with the popper, the winging material is tied in further back from the eye of the hook than when tying the basic 3d streamer.

2 Because this fly is fished deep, it doesn't require the pronounced three-dimensional profile of the 3d streamer. Hence, all of the winging material is tied in conventionally on top of the hook shank.

3 The plastazote head has a slimmer profile than the head for the popper. It needs to provide enough buoyancy to stop the fly from fouling the bottom but not so much that the high-density fly-line will struggle to sink the fly. As with the popper, the head is notched at the back to fit over the dressing. It is fixed with epoxy and is sited high on the hook shank to leave the gape clear.

The double bunny

Dressing

Hook – Partridge, Ad Swier Absolute pike fly hook; size 4/0 or 6/0

Thread – Kevlar

Fins – H2O Fluorofibre

Tail – Two rabbit fur, Magnum Zonker strips and a couple of strands of Flashabou

Under-body – Lureflash UV. Fritz

Winging material – H2O Slinky Fibre

Head – Epoxy

Eyes – Lureflash 3d epoxy eyes 9 mm

The double bunny

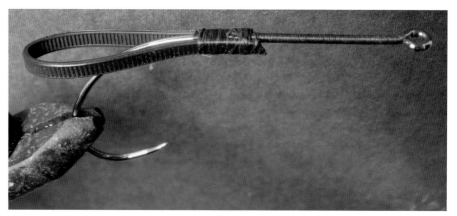

Step 1

1 The rabbit fur strips have an alarming tendency to wrap themselves around the bend of the hook when casting. A projecting loop (I've used a piece of cable tie) tied in above the bend of the hook helps to solve this problem – most of the time!

2 I used to glue the two rabbit fur strips together. This may have produced a fly that was more aesthetically pleasing when out of the water but it also restricted the tail's mobility (a key feature of this fly). When the strips are tied in independently, one on top of the other, skin to skin, they hold together in the water and have a lively wriggle.

The rattler

Dressing

Hook – Partridge, Ad Swier Absolute pike fly hook, size 4/0 or 6/0

Thread – Kevlar

Tail – Two Magnum Zonker strips of rabbit fur

Rattle – Glass tube with two ball-bearings

Under-body – In this example, I've used N.G.D. Dubbing: this has long fibres, attached to a wire flue

Winging Material – H2O Slinky Fibre and Flashabou

Head – Epoxy, finished with nail varnish

Eyes – Rattling 'goggle eyes'

The rattler

1 I use this fly in coloured water conditions so tend to tie it in hi-viz colours, or black.

2 As with the double bunny, I tie in a projecting loop to stop the rabbit fur strips from wrapping themselves around the bend of the hook when casting.

3 The rattle is positioned below the shank with a few loose wraps of Kevlar. It is then tied in securely with tight turns of Kevlar to make it secure. The gap between the shank, Kevlar and rattle is filled with varnish to avoid creating an air pocket which would stop the fly from sinking.

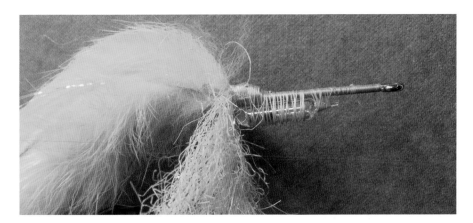

These flies, and variations on them, will solve most fishing problems. Feel free to experiment and tie some monster flies such as Mike Duxbury's large tandem or Andy Bowman's Van the Man. There is a special pleasure to be derived from catching a specimen pike on a fly of your own design and which you have tied yourself.

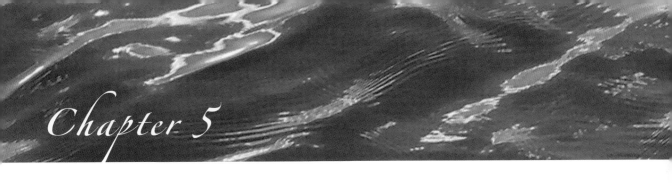

Chapter 5

THE PIKE
FLY-FISHER'S YEAR

W E ANGLERS WHO FLY-FISH for pike are fortunate in that we enjoy three distinct prime times when our sport is at its best. The three times – pre-spawn, post-spawn and the autumn 'stocking up' period – mean that we can fish for pike with confidence for a large part of the year.

Living in rural North Wiltshire means that I am close to a variety of excellent pike waters. The local rivers and my favourite old estate lake operate a close season from 15 March to 15 June which prohibits me from fishing for part of the productive, post-spawn period. This is because the pike is lumped in with the other coarse fish species which spawn later than the pike. Whilst I resent the timing to a degree, I do accept that the pike should be left to spawn in peace and I firmly believe that the quality of fishing benefits from the pike having some respite from our attentions. This is perhaps borne out by the fact that I catch big pike during the opening week more often than not.

In any event, whilst the close season is in force on my local waters, there are other venues to tempt me. Neither Scotland nor Ireland has a close season for pike. They also have stunningly beautiful waters, both large and small, which hardly see an angler all year. Also, during this period, English trout reservoirs will let me fly-fish for pike and I'll often visit Llangorse, a beautiful, natural lake in South Wales.

▲ Winter has lost her grip. I'm hunting for Irish pike with Xavier Lafforgue, fishing through the newly emerging lilies.
(Gardiner Mitchell)

There are two circumstances that will discourage me from fly-fishing for pike. The first, obvious, one is their spawning activity. Apart from the fact that I don't think it's sporting to intrude on the pikes' nuptials, there's the added consideration that, the more successful the pikes' spawning, the more likely it is that I will have splendid pike to fish for in the future. Fortunately, pike in different latitudes tend to operate to different schedules, so I don't need to endure too long a fallow period. The second circumstance can occur during sustained hot weather during the summer. Consistently high temperatures can 'cook' some stillwaters, making the pike lethargic and disinclined to feed. This dour attitude is often connected with (perhaps caused by) low oxygen levels in the water. This in turn means that when a pike – particularly a big fish which takes a long time to land – is caught, it is extremely vulnerable. Too often, a sizeable pike which appears to swim off when released will not survive. Big pike are simply too precious to put them at risk in this way.

High summer temperatures may encourage me to fish for bass off the North Devon coast. Alternatively, I may rest my local stillwaters and fish for pike (plentiful but generally smaller) in well-oxygenated stretches of my local rivers. Another option is to venture further afield and fish the large lochs in Scotland, the large loughs in Ireland or, when the wallet will stand it, the superb lakes of Canada.

Autumn was traditionally the time when English anglers turned their attentions away from other species and concentrated on pike. It wasn't so much that the pike fishing improved as the weather got colder, rather that other fish got harder to catch whilst the pike could be persuaded to take a bait. Autumn can produce superlative pike fishing. Sometimes, the pike will feed vigorously in anticipation of the hard winter conditions to come. As the water cools from the high summer temperatures, it comes to the level at which the pike shake off their summer lethargy. If we're lucky, there will be a cold snap sometime in October to warn the pike that winter is approaching. We will then have a sustained mild spell with cloud cover. The pike will co-operate and we will have sport to savour and tales to tell. Unfortunately, I live in a country which the Weather Gods treat as an amusing playground. Sometimes, autumn seems to get bypassed and we lurch from summer straight into full-blown winter. At other times, early autumn produces torrential rainfall which floods the rivers and turns the lakes into murky places where the pikes' hunting (and thus our fly-fishing) is made more difficult.

Whatever the Weather Gods decide to throw at us, I always look forward to the autumn. I know that there is always the chance of a special day when all the pike in the lake come on simultaneously and hunt, swirling in the shallower water where I can target them easily.

▲ When summer 'cooks' waters at home, you can head to the northern wilderness of Canada. The 'Manitoba sleigh ride' is an exciting experience!

▲ A beautiful bay on a beautiful Scottish loch. When the Weather Gods play fair, autumn can give us good sport in stunning settings. *(Andy Bowman)*

Winter is somewhat unpredictable. Old wives' tales told us that cold weather produced good pike fishing. The traditional pike-fisher's dawn featured a hard frost with crows dropping, frozen to death, from the bare branches. These old wives obviously didn't actually go pike fishing. Yes, pike can be caught in cold weather – I've caught them when most of the lake has been frozen. I've caught them when my casting has been handicapped by lumps of ice forming in my rod rings. As long as the water isn't 'stiff', there is a chance of a pike. That said, masochism should only be practised by masochists. I'm happier to fish in the mild spells that occur during most winters. The pike will feed. They won't feed throughout the day but, if you're tuned in to your water and know the special time when the pike will hunt, then fish can be caught.

During the winter, I lower my expectations. I accept the odd blank session. I'm happy to catch a couple of pike in a session – sometimes, I'm more than happy as a good percentage of the pike caught will be big fish.

◄ The weather was vile and forced us to run the boats ashore and fish the small stretch of available bank. Mark Corps had his spirits lifted by this splendid Irish pike.

At some point, winter relents. At the end of February or early in March (if we're lucky) we'll get some pleasant days. The longer hours of daylight will combine with a slight uplift in temperature to hint that spring is on its way. The pike will be driven by an imperative even more pressing than comfort or hunger. The switch will be thrown that turns their attentions to breeding. They will head to shallow, sheltered bays where the weed-beds will come back to life as the water warms. We will have the chance to fish for pre-spawn pike in specific areas of the lake which makes location easier. This is when the pike are at their heaviest. They are also inclined to feed hungrily prior to the rigours of spawning. The timing of this special fishing is somewhat unpredictable with (so far as I can judge) temperature being a more determining factor than day length. This will produce differences between areas and even marked differences between neighbouring waters.

One of the great pleasures of fly-fishing for pike lies in mastering the range of tactics and techniques that enable you to fish effectively throughout the changing seasons. The pike is a quarry that both warrants and rewards study.

Chapter 6

SPRING TACTICS

LET ME FIRST OF ALL DEFINE what I mean by spring both in terms of time and the pikes' behaviour. I'm referring to the period after the pike have spawned and when they have recovered from their efforts. The weather is noticeably warmer than in the depths of winter and all is right with the world. On my local lakes, I can't start fishing until 16 June but normally, mid-May will see me travelling to waters that I can fish, determined to get the best from this special time.

The most important rule of fly-fishing for pike is a simple one: 'first find your pike'. Therefore, for much of the year, my approach to fly-fishing for pike will be mobile and searching. However, spring helps us with this fundamental matter and at this time of year I will be less mobile and will concentrate my efforts on specific areas that I know from hard-earned experience will be productive. The pike will be in the shallow, weedy bays where they spawned earlier in the year. They will hold in these areas until rising summer temperatures push them into deeper water. This makes the question of location much easier to answer. The pike, including the 'big girls', will be concentrated in specific parts of the lake and will be feeding actively on the coarse fish which converge on these spawning areas after the pike have finished their nuptials. Some simple close-season reconnaissance will pay dividends. Pike, especially big pike, will make their whereabouts pretty obvious at spawning time as they

▲ Andy Bowman and I fished the shallow, reed-fringed bay where the pike had spawned earlier in the year. The lilies were emerging and the rudd and bream had come to perform their nuptials. The pike had come to the restaurant and were keen to feed. Spring pike are lithe, fit and aerobatic. They give your tackle a thorough workout and make the point that they are a top-quality, sporting quarry.

▶ Spring pike are active hunters and give us the chance to enjoy classical, top-of-the-water sport. Seeing a good fish like this nail your fly high in the water gets the adrenalin pumping through the system! (*Andy Bowman*)

crash around in the reeds like active hippos. Taking the trouble to visit the lake when you can't fish it will pay off when the season opens. My dear old dad, now a sprightly nonagenarian, fought at El Alamein during the Second World War. Montgomery, the commander of the British forces, said that time spent in reconnaissance is never time wasted. As with warfare, so with pike fishing!

The warmer water will have cranked up the pikes' metabolic rate, allowing them to digest prey-fish more quickly. This means that not only are the pike keen to feed and put on weight, but they'll do it more frequently. We are less likely to be frustrated by pike we know to be there but can't get to respond. Hungry, feeding pike, that we can find, good weather and clear water, combine to make spring the most productive and most enjoyable season.

Spring is a wonderful time to be on the water. In May 2008, Tim Westcott and I were treated to a splendid display as we fished Eyebrook, a 400 acre trout fishery in Leicestershire. We put our fly-rods down in the boat and just watched as an osprey hovered, soared and dived in majestic style. We didn't object to the competition – we had already caught a few pike! It's also a delight to be there as the whole natural world wakes up. The trees come into leaf, weed-beds grow in the lake, insects hatch and small fish feed. The entire environment moves up a gear and gets on with the business of thriving.

▲ Tim Westbrook and I enjoyed a May session at Eyebrook trout reservoir. We had competition! The osprey treated us to a breathtaking display and caught a small pike. We had brought enough pike to the boat to not feel jealous.

Not only is spring pike fishing productive, it also rewards the use of the most pleasurable techniques. I love to catch pike high in the water. During the spring, I'll use a floating line nearly all the time. My first-choice fly will normally be a slow-sinking, 3d streamer. When the conditions are right, I'll use a popper. I'll fish the shallow bays where the pike spawned earlier in the year. Presenting a fly in relatively shallow water – often no more than 3 ft deep – removes the problem of determining how deep to fish the fly. The water should be reasonably clear. Low rainfall will have prevented the feeder streams from pushing silt into the lake and we should be spared the algal blooms which can turn the water into an unpleasant pea-soup. This means that I will have the chance to sight-fish for pike and can delight in the adrenalin surge that goes with seeing a pike hit my fly.

Whilst locating the right general area to fish can be relatively straight-forward, pinpointing the exact spot where the pike are concentrated requires a degree of watercraft. When I fish Llangorse Lake in Wales during May, I'm confident of finding pike in one area of the lake where the water is quite shallow and the lilies are starting to emerge. However, this 'area' comprises several acres and the pike will not be evenly distributed throughout it. The key to success lies in finding the pikes' restaurant. At 4.00 a.m., when the lake is mirror-calm, this can be simple. I stow my tackle in the boat, start up my stealthy, electric outboard motor and drive out towards the pikes' hunting territory. As I near the right area of the lake, I shut off the motor. I then drift and use the oars to move through the water as quietly and smoothly as possible. My fishing companion hangs over the front of the boat and examines the water carefully, using good yellow-lens Polaroid glasses. When we find the prey-fish, either roach or perch packed in a huge shoal, the mud anchor is slipped over the side. The pike switch on as the light level comes up.

On a perfect morning, we'll be treated to some great entertainment. There will be sprays of prey-fish jumping clear of the water, followed by violent swirls as the pike hunt in earnest. The fishing technique is straightforward. A 3d streamer, tied to suggest the species of prey-fish, is fished alongside or below the shoal which is now high in the water, dimpling the surface. If a pike swirls within casting range, the fly is quickly banged into the ensuing ripple and allowed to sink for a few seconds. A slow, erratic retrieve usually results in a savage take and a lively pike tries to drag you out of the boat.

In May 2008 my guiding client, Jonathan Simmons, and I took nearly a hundred pike, including some good double-figure fish, in two days. May the previous year gave my client and me a haul of twenty-three pike before midday in a single session. On that occasion, the pike were feeding on perch.

You won't get that many chances to enjoy such frantic sport in a year, so take advantage of every opportunity that presents itself. The key is to be alive to what is happening around you. Fortunately, during the spring, the pike will often give the game away. Also, good feeding spells aren't punctuated by longer periods of inactivity. At this time of year, the pike will feed more often. With metabolism in overdrive, they will digest a belly full of roach more quickly than at other times.

The tactics mentioned above work on most large, natural stillwaters. As I said earlier, it definitely helps to be familiar with the lake you are fishing. Certainly, you can use your knowledge of pike behaviour as a sensible starting point when you are looking for fish. However, on every water, there will be specific areas which consistently produce more and larger pike than others.

On smaller lakes, this phenomenon can be quite pronounced. A particular bay and the water surrounding it will produce superb results every spring. Another, seemingly identical, bay will prove much less fruitful. The angler prepared to put in the time and effort to accumulate knowledge will enjoy better results than the angler who flits from venue to venue, hoping that a water will yield up its secrets instantly. Pike can be harsh mistresses but they reward the attentive, persistent suitor.

It's undoubtedly worth the effort. For several years now, I have enjoyed spectacular spring pike fishing on several waters that I have taken the trouble to get to know well. I bitterly regret that, in the past, I didn't realise how good this fishing could be. I stuck to the old English close season and missed out on the fabulous sport I could have enjoyed had I focused my attentions on waters in Scotland, Ireland, Wales or indeed the Swedish Baltic. For many years, I restricted my spring pike fishing to the old estate lake near my home. Most years, this meant that I enjoyed a short period of very good sport. However, some years, I missed out. Sometimes, the Weather Gods conspired against me. By the time the season opened on 16 June, the special spring fishing opportunity was gone and I was faced with the altogether less favourable option of summer pike fishing. By casting my attentions further afield, I have been able to enjoy a much longer period of special spring fishing.

Although, in May, I have to travel to catch pike, from 16 June onward I can concentrate on my local waters. The long hours of daylight mean that I have lots of fishing time available. I can slot in a few hours at my local lake before breakfast and can indulge my passion without totally neglecting domestic issues. The fishing is too good resist. I do some guiding work – I need to earn a crust and try to justify my somewhat selfish lifestyle to my family – but I also have some 'personal' fishing sessions when I lose myself in the beauty of my surroundings and just concentrate on catching pike.

On 18 June 2007, Mike Duxbury came with me for a guided fishing session. I think he was surprised when I told him that we were going to leave the boat in the lake's boathouse and restrict our fishing to a single, small bay. We fished from the bank, covering no more than one hundred yards. We caught pike, lots of pike, big pike. Mike's session was topped by a splendid fish of 24 lb. We finished with aching arms and smiling faces. We had caught a large number of sizeable pike from a surprisingly small area because we had been stealthy, taking care not to spook fish by clumsy casting or advertising our presence. We had fished patiently, resting the water after taking a fish. We had continued to catch because we hadn't just caught a couple of pike and moved on. Had we done so, we would have missed out on a spectacular haul.

On that occasion, we were fortunate. The weather stayed pleasantly cool and the sun stayed behind the clouds. The pike fed throughout the day. You won't always have such convenient conditions. Often, if you want to enjoy a haul of spring pike, you will have to steel yourself to abandon your warm bed whilst it's still dark and your fuddled brain requires a hefty dose of strong coffee to spark into life. You will drive to the water in the dark and will assemble your tackle as the first fingers of light are brightening the eastern sky. You will be fishing by 5.00 a.m. You may be rewarded with a pike immediately, or you may have to be patient until the rising sun has burnt off the mist. Typically, these sunny days will produce good sport up to mid-morning. The fishing will then tail off: from midday until early evening, the pike will switch off. On some days, there will be another flurry of activity as dusk falls. If you want to take advantage of both of these feeding periods, you are faced with a long day's fishing – from 5.00 a.m. until after 10.00 p.m., even longer in Scotland or the Swedish Baltic. You can, however, take a break during the middle of the day without worrying too much about missing chances. If I have to choose between fishing the morning and the evening, I would normally vote for the morning session. It offers a longer productive period and is generally the more reliable. I think the pike have plenty of available prey-fish in the morning, hunt with enthusiasm, fill their bellies and digest their meal. It can be the following morning before they feed actively again. The angler who shuts off the alarm clock, rolls over and enjoys a lie-in can miss the best of the fishing.

▼ Sometimes, when the days are long, you need to be on the water early to coincide with the pikes' mealtime. There are compensations. The lough is inspiringly beautiful when its surface is mirror-glass calm and painted by the low, early sun.
(Andy Bowman)

As previously mentioned, I catch most of my early morning spring pike by fishing a 3d streamer with a floating line. The flies which prove most consistently successful are those tied to suggest the predominant species of prey-fish in the lake, but sometimes the pike can surprise us in this regard. During the very productive session (which I've referred to previously) on Llangorse in May 2008, Jonathan Simmons and I were catching plenty of pike, including the odd nice double-figure fish, by using perch imitation flies. I then connected with a small pike of about 3 lb which I began to haul in without too much care. I felt an alarming thump on the end of my line and my leader was broken instantly: a big pike had decided to eat the jack that had taken my fly.

A couple of weeks later, I was fishing a 'secret lough' in Ireland with Andy Bowman. We were catching pike on conventional 3d streamers but felt that our results were falling short of the lough's undoubted potential. A couple of months previously, I had enjoyed some encouraging sport on the water, connecting with several sizeable pike. Andy is renowned for tying some crazy pike flies. He produced something from his tackle bag which looked like it needed a diet of Brazil nuts. Along each side of the large fly, he had tied feather slips of olive with yellow markings. The fly made a very passable imitation of a jack pike. He started to catch pike more consistently. He gave me one and my catch rate also improved. The following morning, we were on the lough at first light. Andy retrieved his fly along a wall of ranunculus and we watched in amazement as the green leaves parted and a huge pike came out to investigate. The water was crystal clear and we were tingling with anticipation. The pike's fins gave a tell-tale quiver and in a click of the fingers, she had accelerated, as only a pike can, engulfed the fly, turned and tried to drag Andy out of the boat. The ensuing battle was spectacular. The pike made a succession of arm-wrenching runs, treated us to a wild aerobatic display and fought as only an Irish pike can, before Andy brought her over the net.

Andy christened the fly pattern 'Van the Man'. We had been listening to Van Morrison on the car's stereo so it seemed appropriate. The choice of fly certainly had a bearing on our success rate. Unfortunately it had one

▼ The pain of prising ourselves out of our beds was rewarded. I'm no great shakes as a photographer but was lucky enough to catch Andy's 23 lb pike trying to convince us she was a tarpon. The 'secret lough' produced several splendid pike for us that morning – Andy's 'Van the Man' fly proved its worth.

distinct disadvantage. The feather slips which made it such a convincing jack pike imitation didn't stand up to the pikes' teeth. The half dozen examples that Andy had brought with him were chomped beyond recognition by the end of the second day's fishing. I have since tried to produce a similar effect, using more robust synthetic materials. My version is certainly more durable but it takes far longer to produce as it involves much fiddly work with dyes and marker pens. (Having subsequently looked through the photographs of our trip, I realise that I was trying to solve a problem that didn't exist. I hadn't registered just how many big pike had hit Andy's original fly.)

Whichever option one chooses, a jack pike imitation is well worth including in one's fly box for spring fishing. During the pre-spawn period, small, male pike have the enviable status of husband. Come the spring, post-spawn period, they are relegated to 'lunch'. Coarse fishers too have recognised that a jack can be a successful bait for a big pike.

Andy regaled me with tales of how he had used his 'Van the Man' pattern on Loch Awe in Scotland for pre-spawn fishing. It hadn't proved particularly successful but had been followed by several big girls. He was convinced that the big female pike were more interested in having sex with his fly than with nailing it.

▼ It was the tooth marks across the back of this sweet little pike that prompted us to switch to Andy's jack pike imitating fly. (Andy Bowman)

◀ 'Van the Man' – not for boys! Hard work to cast but we didn't care. The string of big pike that it produced meant that we were high on adrenalin and casting like Olympians! *(Andy Bowman)*

Spring (usually!) gives us the benefit of clear water conditions. The pike can see our fly from a considerable distance, which greatly improves our chances. It also means that imitative patterns fill most of the space in my fly-box. Clear water gives us the chance of the most enjoyable fly-fishing that anyone can ask for. Sight fishing for big pike is as good as it gets. Although pike aren't at their top weight in the spring, we have two distinct advantages. The first is that we can locate the big pike. The second is that they are at their most willing to hit our fly.

Prior to some recent successes, the biggest pike that I had ever caught took my fly one morning in June 2004. I had woken early to find that it was hammering down with rain. Normally, this would discourage me from going pike fishing. I have never had success in heavy rain – I suspect that the clatter of raindrops on the surface of the lake interferes with the pikes' sensory systems and they wait until they can hunt more efficiently. However, for some reason, I clawed my way out of bed, threw some clothes on and put the roof up on my old roadster. I drove to the lake with a feeling of optimism. I just had a feeling that the rain would stop and something special would happen. True enough, by the time it was light enough to tackle up, the air was clear and still. I crimped a 7 in rudd streamer onto my wire trace, hooked the fly into the keeper ring on my rod and set off across the fields. The air was laden with the fragrance of fresh, wet grass and my wellingtons left a tell-tale trail as I walked. I knew where the pike were, having had some good sport – including a 20 lb fish – earlier in the week.

The edge of the lake was fringed with reeds. Every fifty yards or so, the reeds had been cut through and wooden fishing stages gave access to the bay. The surface of the lake was mirror-calm and undisturbed by any signs of fish moving. I made a couple of short casts from a kneeling position behind the first stage. Satisfied that there wasn't a pike under my toes, I cautiously made my way onto the wooden platform and started to put out longer casts in an arc to cover the water. I fished out the first area without any response, hitched my tackle bag onto my shoulder and made my way to the next stage. The sun had risen far enough to allow some light into the water and let me view the channels in the weed-growth. A few bream were cruising slowly through the water. At least the restaurant was open – I strained my eyes to try to spot a customer. She was lying stationary in water, just 3 ft deep, that was clear enough for me to be able to make out every one of her primrose spots. She was huge – almost certainly bigger than any pike I had caught. I unhitched my fly and pulled enough line off my reel to allow me to cover her. Despite the fact that my heart was thumping with impatience, I took the trouble to carefully arrange the coils of fly-line so that they wouldn't tangle in mid-cast. I took a deep breath and aerialised some line. Two false casts, a final smooth haul and I shot my line. The Gods were kind. Despite my nervousness, the cast was perfect and delivered my streamer 10 ft in front and 10 ft beyond where she lay, still motionless. The fibres in the heavily dressed fly trapped air and it sat up on the flat surface of the water. I didn't move a hair for what felt like an hour (it was probably less than a minute). Gingerly, and oh so slowly, I tightened my line until I was tight to my fly. I was sure she had spotted it. I gave one short, firm tug to sink the fly. Wham! The pike moved with invisible speed. I didn't need to react as my rod was yanked around savagely. I stripped with my left hand to make sure that my hook was pulled home and just held on as the drag on my reel squealed. She was heading for the reeds against the opposite bank – I laid my rod over and applied as much side-strain as my 9 weight rod would withstand. I'm not really sure whether I succeeded in turning her or whether she just decided to head for open water. There was quite a lot of backing through my tip ring and I certainly didn't feel as though I was in control. Every time she charged off, I had to let her take line. Every time she came towards me, I tried to get line back onto my reel. I knew it would be dangerous to have yards of fly-line wafting around my feet. After ten minutes (I had looked at my watch) things started to slow down. She circled in front of me and I kept as much pressure on her as possible. I felt giddy, almost sick with tension as I started to try to pump her slowly towards me. She came, just a few feet for each pull with my rod. I knew that when she saw me she would explode so tried to tire her, without rushing to get her over the net. I'd had her on for fifteen minutes and decided to bring her close. Sure enough, when she saw the net, she made another, unstoppable, head-shaking run. I was out of breath and my right bicep was screaming with pain but suddenly I started to feel confident. This run was shorter – my backing stayed on the reel. We went through the same routine three more times. Each time, although I couldn't stop her taking line, her runs were shorter. I tried to get my breathing under control. My rod bent all the way as I pumped her towards the net. The whole process felt as if it was in slow motion. As she came towards the sunken net, I had a flicker of panic – was the net big enough? The question was answered as I lifted and she slid inside the pear-shaped frame – she was in! I put my rod down on the stage and got both of my hands on the frame of the landing net. I carried my prize to the bank, laid her carefully on the long wet grass and let out a whoop of delight that must have been heard throughout Wiltshire. Unhooking was quick and simple. I hooked my scales into the weigh sling and watched the dial keep going round. At 32 lb 4 oz she was a monster – the biggest pike I had ever landed. I hung over the wooden stage, supporting her in the water for a few minutes until she kicked and was gone. I was high on adrenalin.

There is a cautionary rider to this tale. After regaining my composure, I picked up my rod. I looked around the surface of the bay. There was another pike, every bit as large as the fish I had just landed. Again, the cast was spot on. Again the pike took savagely. Here, the two tales diverge. Instead of the exhilarating surge of a powerful pike, there was a heart-rending crack as my leader broke. I know that I should have checked my tackle thoroughly before making another cast. The excitement had just proved too much for me. It was a hard way to have the lesson rammed home.

I caught a couple more pike, including a fish of 11 lb that was grabbed by another huge pike. She let it go after dragging it around the bay for a couple of minutes. The smaller fish swam off strongly enough after I had unhooked it but it had an alarming set of teeth marks across its back. I'll never know whether the attacker was the same fish that I had lost earlier or a third monster pike. My casting became clumsy. My ability to concentrate evaporated. It was time to head for home. I walked slowly back to my car and stowed my tackle in the boot. I drove with the roof down and enjoyed the cooling breeze. Life was good.

Since that memorable morning, I have caught seven more pike weighing over 30 lb. All have been spring fish.

Guiding clients often ask me how they can tell when they have got a take. In truth, the pike will make it pretty obvious! However, knowing your fly has been hit by a pike is one thing; securing a firm hook-hold is another matter altogether. Beginners usually get it wrong a few times before they start to connect with any consistency. The first problem is that takes from pike can be too exciting. In the spring, the pike will often take your fly high in the water. The visual shock is wonderful but it often triggers an instantaneous, rod-wafting strike, which only succeeds in pulling the fly out of the pike's jaws.

The solution is to stay cool. Imagine, the pike takes the fly from behind and turns. You need to strike after the pike has turned. Merely giving a half-hearted pull with your fly-rod won't set a 4/0 hook home – pike have hard, bony mouths. I use the same technique as tarpon fishers, stripping line back with my left hand, then pulling my rod into the fish. It takes a fair bit of 'grunt' to set a big hook. It is better to hook the pike with this 'strip-strike' method and then take advantage of the cushioning effect of the fly-rod. You need to be careful when you get a savage take from a big pike at very close range – sometimes with no fly-line out through your tip ring. An over-vigorous strike with the rod, at the same time as a 20 lb fish is accelerating in the opposite direction, can result in a broken rod. It's better to lower your rod, strip-strike and then pull into the fish with your rod. This paragraph was easy to write. Sometimes, it's hard to stay cool when you have just seen several feet of green and gold appear from nowhere and nail your fly in less time than it takes to click your fingers.

The best way to learn how to hook pike consistently is to practise by getting lots of pike to take your fly. The more you get the chance to practise, the better your percentage of hook-ups will become. Even the best and most experienced pike fly-fishers have days when they struggle to connect with takes. Mike Duxbury has experimented with tying flies with circle hooks attached as stingers after experiencing a couple of particularly frustrating sessions. (A 'stinger' is a small hook attached to a trailing length of wire tied along the shank of the main fly-hook. It is then right at the tail of the fly. The idea is that it will hook a pike that is just nipping at the tail of the fly.) He still had takes which didn't 'stick' and has abandoned the experiment. On the good days, when you have mastered the technique, most of your takes will result in securely hooked pike.

In the spring you can sometimes experience particularly aggravating takes. They happen when the pike are in a real feeding frenzy. You are retrieving your fly, there is a violent wallop as the pike hits it – then nothing. You can

sometimes overcome this problem by having 'soft hands' and gently yielding to the take before tightening and setting the hook firmly as you retrieve. Another effective option is to retrieve with your rod tip three or four feet above the water. Generally, I retrieve with my rod tip almost touching the water, since this prevents the fly-line bouncing on the surface and setting up tell-tale ripples. However, if you are suffering from split-second, violent wallops on your fly then the 'slack' bow in the line that you have when holding the rod up can solve the problem.

▲ The bow in the line below a high rod can give you a 'cushion' when you are expecting savage, 'banging' takes.

Poppers come into their own in the spring. I think that every pike fly-fisher who has achieved a reasonable level of competence and confidence should be compelled to fish with a popper until this method has produced a few pike. To the uninitiated, it can seem too outlandish a technique to offer any chance of success. The angler who lacks confidence will blank, whereas the person convinced that it will produce a pike usually gets the desired result. Don't ask me to explain this phenomenon – just trust me!

I have described how to fish the popper in Chapter 3. In this chapter, I would like to extol the benefits of fishing poppers in the spring. They work best in quite specific conditions. (I'm sure that some people will disagree with my theories and opinions on when, how, where and why to use a popper. I can only present my own experiences and explain how poppers have worked for me.) The most crucial condition that needs to be met is flat-calm water. We often get this at dawn and dusk, in May and June. Poppers work well enough at first light but it is in the evening that they can give you an edge. I'll offer up my theory as to why this should be so.

In the morning, whilst poppers can catch pike, a 3d streamer will usually give better results. I think this is because a fly which more closely imitates a prey-fish is more likely to be hit by a pike that is intent on eating prey-fish. However, a pike that has achieved a full belly and is quietly digesting its meal is a different proposition. With such a fish, you need to provoke a reaction, rather than trigger a feeding response. A popper can provoke a reaction.

In May 2008 I took Jon Graham out on Llangorse. He had arrived at mid-morning and we planned to fish late into the dusk, get a few hours' sleep, and return at the crack of dawn. Fishing through the afternoon produced the odd pike but nothing of any note. As the light faded the breeze dropped and the surface of the lake turned to polished plate glass. I suggested that Jon should try a popper. I explained how to fish it and took the boat in, close to the lilies. Jon cast the popper into tiny inlets in the lily-bed. After a couple of attempts he was probably convinced that I was merely 'jollying him along'. Then he had a take. He had been twitching his fly across the surface without the slightest indication that there was a pike within a hundred yards of his offering. Suddenly there was an eruption under his popper and a big fish (certainly more than 20 lb) exploded into the air with his fly in its jaws. Jon couldn't restrain himself. The instinctive, immediate strike just plucked the fly away from the pike.

Jon was disappointed but commendably philosophical. At least he had experienced the excitement of seeing a big pike's aerobatic skills. I apologised. I had explained how to fish the popper but hadn't explained how to connect with a take. When a pike takes from below and launches itself into the air, you have to wait until the pike has hit the water and is heading away from you. I consoled Jon by explaining that a pike you have missed on a popper may well come again. It did. The second take was every bit as dramatic as the first. Water sprayed everywhere as the big pike took off. Jon stayed cool. He did everything right but the hook didn't go home. I tried to console Jon. I told him how my son Sebastian had come up with a great expression: 'Have you spooked it or just annoyed it?' Jon had just annoyed it. The third take was amazing – another explosion of white water as the big pike went airborne again. This time Jon connected. His rod bucked round as more than a yard of very aggravated pike decided to show him who was the boss. Sadly, this story doesn't have a happy ending (for Jon that is!). After a frantic scrap lasting five minutes, the hook came adrift. Jon stood up in the boat, slammed his rod down and swore loudly and with real passion. It shocked the party of elderly ladies who were ensconced in the nearby bird hide. I felt for him. To lose a good fish like that is desperately disappointing. The pike didn't come again. This time, it had been spooked.

Nevertheless, I'm sure that Jon is now convinced that poppers work and will take delight in catching pike on the surface. He is a good angler. Rather than just being disappointed at losing a big pike, he had the fortitude to be pleased to have discovered a technique that would stand him in good stead for the future.

Andy Smith, who runs the Hardy's Instructors Academy, likened popper fishing for pike to tarpon fishing and rated it as every bit as exciting (and much less expensive!). Tarpon anglers tend to measure their success by the number of fish 'jumped' rather than the number of fish landed. Anyone who is adventurous enough to fish for pike with a popper will miss some takes and will have some fish come adrift. They will also have as much adrenalin-pumping excitement as any healthy heart can cope with. On the good days every take will stick and the angler will go home in a state of delirium, needing to lie down in a darkened room until normal pulse rate has been restored.

Fly-fishing for pike in the spring is quite simply the best sport that a freshwater angler can experience. If you are a dyed-in-the-wool trout fisher, considering flirting with pike fishing (but only later in the year) I would urge you to give it a go. I too once confined my pike fishing to the autumn and the winter. Now, I'm obsessed and rate the spring as the most enjoyable and productive time to fish for pike.

Chapter 7

SUMMER TACTICS

IT'S A SHAME THAT PIKE fishing isn't at its best during the long, hot days of summer. The post-spawn certainties evaporate as the pike disperse, leaving the shallow, weedy bays. You notice a decline as your spring fishing tactics produce fewer pike and smaller pike. It's time to ring the changes. 'Changes' can mean fishing different areas of the lake. It can mean fishing deeper in the water with different flies. I'll often forsake my favourite, floating fly-line and instead use a slow-sinking, intermediate line or a fast-sinking shooting head.

The 'change' can be quite fundamental. If the summer is hot and settled, I may well switch my attentions from my familiar old estate lake and opt to fish on the rivers, where the well-oxygenated, cooler water will contain more co-operative pike. I may also travel to fish a large Irish lough or a Scottish loch, less affected by the summer conditions.

I once thought that I knew the trigger which moved us from spring to summer fishing. At my local estate lake, when the water temperature hit 17 °C, the big female pike deserted the shallows and I had to pursue them in other parts of the lake. I naïvely assumed that this would apply on other lakes. Then, a few years ago, I was enjoying wonderful spring sport on Llangorse. Every morning, before heading off in the boat, I diligently dunked my thermometer in the water. On one occasion, I recorded a reading of 16 °C and duly motored off to fish along the edge of the lilies where I had been catching good pike.

▶ The calendar is less important than the temperature. Andy Bowman took this cracking July pike from a Scottish loch when conditions in England were much less encouraging.

▼ Terry Jackson, a well known Irish specimen hunter, fishes a favourite Irish lough from a belly-boat. Although such waters warm up less than many others, it's definitely more pleasurable when the water temperature isn't chilling your extremities! (Andy Bowman)

I couldn't find a pike. In desperation, I moved and ran my fly along a steeper drop-off, adjacent to a reed-bed. I caught three good fish quickly and a couple more from similar spots during the course of the morning. I now realise that the 'trigger' may not be water temperature as such but, rather, the behaviour of the pikes' prey-fish. (Perhaps temperature relative to latitude or weather trends may also have some influence.) As always, a theory can be a useful starting point but is never a substitute for detailed, local knowledge.

In the spring, I am often able to cover productive water from the bank or by careful wading. At my local estate lake, during the summer, I am reduced to a couple of hundred yards of bank that let me cast my fly into deeper water. This may be fine for a quick, two-hour session at first light but seriously restricts the percentage of the lake's pike population that I can fish for. During the summer months, most of my stillwater pike fishing will be from a boat. Generally, I'll look to fish deeper water. This can mean that I'm hunting for the same number of pike over a much wider area than in the spring. To improve my odds of locating pike, I'll look for reasons for them to be in particular places. These reasons can include cover and the presence of prey-fish. The dam wall is a regular pike-catching spot. On a hot summer's day in 2007, my guiding client Mike Duxbury took four big double-figure pike in a short spell whilst fishing from a boat. We were anchored in deep water about thirty yards from the wall, which can't be fished from the bank. Mike is an impressive caster and was able to clip the wall with his big streamer pattern. The explosive takes occurred within a few seconds as the pike were lying tight against the wall. On our way back to the boathouse, we fished an 18 ft deep hole which regularly houses some big pike in the summer. We were fishing with slow-sinking, intermediate lines and had a couple of good fish by working our streamers slowly and deep in the water. There was a huge swirl on the surface as a pike sent half a dozen rudd scattering out of the water. Mike had seen the commotion and immediately cast his fly into the middle of the expanding ripples. Instead of letting his fly sink, the method that had brought success previously, he started to retrieve straight away and was rewarded with a fabulous surface take that resulted in another big double-figure pike.

We had enjoyed a successful day but realised that our success had owed little to luck. Most of our fish had been caught because we had identified the right parts of the lake. Mike's 'bonus' pike had been caught because he tunes in to the water. He had spotted a feeding pike and had used the right technique.

It always pays to be observant. In calm summer conditions, it can often seem as if all the pike have gone on holiday. Tuning in to the water can help you to catch a pike when it seemed as if you were doomed to failure. Look out for sedges hatching. They will often encourage rudd to feed high in the water which, in turn, can stimulate the pike to feed. Look out for sea birds taking fry off the surface. Sometimes, the small fish are high in the water because there is a big pike underneath them. Fishing a fly below the massed shoal of fry can sometimes provoke a response from a pike that just can't be bothered to come up in the water to harry the tiddlers. In the summer, the pike are likely to be less active and the angler in tune with the surroundings can sometimes take a fish or two and turn failure into satisfying success.

It's very rare for me to fish all day during summer. The pike don't normally feed furiously throughout the day. It's far better to fish at the times when the pike are more likely to be active. Early and late is the best strategy. If I can't do both, then I prefer an early morning session to a late evening one. The early morning generally offers a longer opportunity. The late evening session will often become productive only when the light has almost gone. I have caught pike after dark – sometimes on surface poppers, which is extremely exciting. However, most of the waters I fish don't allow night fishing and unhooking a big pike in the dark can be challenging.

In the summer, my first choice method will often be a big, 3d streamer or a double bunny fished on a slow-sinking, intermediate line. This will enable me to fish my fly slowly, in deeper water, further down in the water than I would in the spring. Often enough, this will produce a fish or two. It works when the pike, if not quite on the rampage, are at least willing to follow and hit the fly. On some days, however, it becomes a monotonous sequence of retrieves that elicits no response from the pike. On such days, the pike are glued to the bottom of the lake and just can't be persuaded to burn calories and chase your fly. These days call for a different technique.

I know that I'm repeating myself but the golden rule of fly-fishing for pike is 'first find your pike'. At most times of the year, getting this fundamental point right will assure you of some success. During the dog-days of summer, you may have to add another phrase: 'then pull your fly past its nose'. To achieve this, I will often resort to the heavy artillery. I will change my spool for one loaded with a high-density shooting head (a sink rate of 8 in per second). I will use a buoyant, bomber fly, a wire trace and a short, 3 ft leader. I'll put out a long cast and allow my line to sink, letting out some slack so that there is no pendulum effect to foreshorten my cast. The weight of the shooting head will sink my buoyant fly and tether it close to the bottom of the lake. I'll then work the bomber back towards me, slowly and erratically, pulling it down as I retrieve and letting it flutter up in the water when I pause. This allows me to fish the bottom of the lake where the pike are lurking. It's a slow, painstaking process and my casting fan will contain more casts than when I'm fishing for pike that will chase my fly. Slow and painstaking it may be; it also works. It can produce a take when other methods were merely giving you casting practice. The take may be a good positive pull, it may just be a feeling that your line has got 'heavy'.

Whatever sort of take you get, it's essential that you strip the bow out of your line, connect with the pike and keep the pressure on. Don't let the high-density shooting head drown your line. If this happens and you're not in straight line contact with the pike, then it's likely that your fly will come adrift. Takes are too hard to come by to lose a pike through poor playing technique.

If I'm boat fishing and I'm confident that I'm in the right place, I prefer to fish at anchor. This allows me to work my fly as slowly as possible and gives me the best chance of a response from a pike. However, there are plenty of times, particularly when fishing reservoirs, when I'm far from confident. On these occasions, I may well opt to drift – often using a drogue to slow the boat's progress – and cover more water. You need to decide whether it is better to cover fewer pike more methodically or more pike in a more cursory fashion.

Often, the pike that you land through this technique will have leeches on them. This is a sure sign that they have been inactive on the bed of the lake rather than actively hunting.

The English summer is unpredictable. Your pike-fishing efforts will meet with more success if you tailor your approach to the prevailing conditions. Because of this, I'm reluctant to make firm plans a long time in advance. I know that during cooler spells I may well be able to catch pike with reasonable consistency around drop-offs on my local stillwaters. Sometimes, early in the summer, we can experience fishing that is halfway between the spring sport and the more difficult summer fishing. Sometimes, there will still be some pike close to the areas they occupied in the spring. However, they are unlikely to feed as vigorously as they did a few weeks earlier. When you are faced with this situation, an early morning raid with a popper may give surprisingly good results. In July 2005, I had a splendid dawn session – four good pike topped by a cracker of 21 lb 8 oz. The second heaviest fish was about the same weight when I hooked it but spat out a 2 lb bream before being netted! I was only able to fish for an hour and a half that morning as I was providing the obligatory parental taxi service to get my young son to a football tournament he was playing in. I had struggled over the previous few sessions when using a conventional 3d streamer. I enjoyed a few more productive dawn raids with a popper before the pike decamped to their summer quarters. I think that the popper gave me more success than a streamer because it was more provocative. The summer pike may not feed so actively but they can still be aggravated!

I know that, on occasions, I will have to fish the deeper holes. I also know that if the lakes are cooked, I will probably enjoy better sport on the rivers. I'm fortunate in having several good stretches of river within a half-hour drive of my home. One productive beat is within ten minutes of my front door. This is a fortunate situation but it's far from unique. In England, anyone living outside of the urban sprawl is likely to be close to a river that holds pike.

River pike are, on average, smaller than their stillwater brethren. However, whilst the general run of pike will be smaller, many rivers do yield up the odd big fish and often the pike are quite plentiful. During the summer, the rivers offer many advantages.

In the first instance, the pike are less likely to be dour. Water temperatures and oxygen levels are less likely to be a problem. Weirpools can be particularly good spots to target. However, it's important to be mobile. Some ideal spots will regularly produce a pike; other, seemingly identical, swims will be unproductive.

▶ This Thames weirpool with its well-oxygenated water is a favourite haunt for summer pike.

During the summer, transferring our attentions from stillwaters to smaller rivers can give an encouraging boost to our confidence. Even if the pike aren't in a feeding frenzy, at least we can cover them. And, if we can cover them, we at least have a chance of inducing a response. In order to cover the fish, we may well need the ability to present our fly at different depths. Rather than mess around with different lines, I prefer to have a small spool of heavy, lead-substitute wire in my pocket. A few turns of this, wound onto the under-body behind the wing of my fly, can enable me to fish with more control. I'm always happier when I'm fishing my fly as I want to, rather than at the speed, depth and run dictated by the river.

Fly-fishing for pike in the summer faces us with some questions of ethics. Low oxygen levels and high water temperatures make pike vulnerable. Because they are such strong, hard-fighting fish, some anglers assume that they are indestructible. Not so – pike are surprisingly fragile. Because of this, it's vital that we look to cause them as little stress as possible.

Summer pike should be played firmly and landed as quickly as possible. I stress again the importance of using barbless, single hooks to minimise the time taken to unhook the pike. Whenever possible, I remove the fly without removing the pike from the water. You don't need to spend time photographing summer pike – you should have a veritable gallery of pictures from your

◄ Returning pike as quickly as possible is crucial in the summer. I unhooked Michael Hofmeyr's good fish in the water. The big, barbless hook made it simple and the pike was supported until she swam off strongly. Take your 'hero shots' in the spring or the autumn. In the summer, cause the pike as little stress as possible. *(Michael Hofmeyr)*

spring sport and you'll catch plenty more fish during the autumn. It's important to release summer pike carefully. Simply flicking out your fly and letting the pike sink down into the lake isn't the way to do it. The pike should be supported until it kicks strongly and swims away, having recovered fully.

If you are happy that conditions are acceptable, catch some pike and enjoy your fishing. If the summer is a scorcher or there are de-oxygenating algal blooms on the lake, show the pike the respect they deserve and leave them in peace.

When faced with such conditions in the middle of summer, I check the tide tables. This is when I head for the coast of north Devon and use my pike fly-fishing equipment in the sea. Big bass don't excite me quite as much as pike but they are an entertaining, sporting quarry. A word of caution – saltwater can destroy fishing tackle. My rod and reel are designed for use in the sea but I still

▶ Sometimes summer will see me in pursuit of other species. Bass may not excite me as much as pike but they are a lively sporting quarry and can provide plenty of entertainment when the pike are dour. My friend, Jim Hendrick is a top bass fishing guide from Wexford in Ireland – he's also a great pike fly-fisher.

wash them thoroughly with fresh water after my fishing session. I once made the mistake of lending a thoughtless angler an old fly-reel to use for bass fishing. The end result was a nasty corroded mess that was would never again be of any use for catching fish. By way of further precaution I tend to re-spool a saved old line when I'm fishing from rocks. It's also a good idea to take a line tray. Having a beautiful, expensive new fly-line shredded by the waves battering it against sharp rocks is not a good plan.

Most years, July, August and September are (apart from April when I leave them alone, to spawn and recover in peace) my least productive months for pike. Don't be despondent! These months can also be hard for the trout fisherman. 'Least productive' isn't the same as pointless. Usually, by being selective about where, when and how I fish, I can catch enough pike to keep things interesting. There are compensations too. Early morning by a lake or river is a fascinating time to observe wildlife. Most of the waters that I fish are hosts to electric-blue kingfishers. They are a cheering sight, even when the fishing is slow. Many times during the summer, I have been delighted to watch deer come down to drink from the lake. The summer may not give me my most successful pike fishing but it provides thoroughly enjoyable times in beautiful surroundings. I shouldn't complain too loudly!

Chapter 8

AUTUMN TACTICS

I get impatient during the summer. Clear blue skies, high temperatures and mirror-calm lakes are fine for picnics. My teenage daughter enjoys showing off her great legs and wearing flattering clothes. My legs are hairy, white and somewhat knobbly – not a pretty sight. My wardrobe contains robust weather-beating country clothing.

I get impatient for the weather to cool and for the pike to switch on. The trigger is the definite change from summer to autumn. In a good year, this will be precipitated by a short, chilly snap in October followed by settled, mild weather with water temperatures holding at between 10 and 12 °C. If we are lucky, some colour will drop out of the water and the oxygen levels will increase. The right conditions will spark a dramatic improvement in our pike-fishing prospects.

When this happens, I no longer have to bump my fly along the bottom in deeper parts of the lake. The pike are no longer 'lurking' – now, they are hunting along the drop-offs. I, in turn, can now hunt them with my fly-rod, confident that my efforts will be rewarded.

For the coarse fisherman, autumn is traditionally the start of the pike-fishing season. For me, it's one of the three prime times to fish for pike. For the all-round fly-fisher, it can provide challenging and exciting fishing when the seasons for wild trout and salmon have drawn to a close. Whilst the pike will

► In the autumn, the pike will often reveal their location as they hunt actively, scattering prey-fish and producing tell-tale swirls on the surface. A fly cast into the ebbing rings of such a swirl will often produce an immediate, solid take. *(Michael Hofmeyr)*

be more active than in the summer, they will be less defined in their locations than in the spring. That isn't to say that they will be more evenly distributed, rather that the potential catching spots will be more numerous. This means that we should be mobile and observant. Pike will be in particular places for specific reasons. These 'reasons' will be food supply and hunting cover.

Sometimes, we can use our ability to read the water, to identify good spots to target. I regularly fish a stretch of The King's Sedgemoor Drain on the Somerset Levels. There is a place where a feeder drain enters the main river with a weir gate that regulates the flow of water. It creates a pocket of slack water where the pike herd huge numbers of prey-fish – the perfect fish-trap. In the autumn, the died-back lily bed in front of the feeder's mouth provides the pike with cover. The combination means that it's a rare session when a few pike can't be tempted to take a fly.

Location is the single most important factor for catching pike in the autumn. You don't need to rely just on your own efforts. If you are fishing a river, talk to the coarse match fishermen. They'll know where the prey-fish are holding. They'll know where pike have grabbed the plump roach that they have hooked. Even the stillwater pike-fishers who sit and wait for their fish-baits to be gobbled can be helpful. The dead-bait anglers at my local estate lake seem to regard me as a harmless eccentric rather than a competitor and will often supply me with invaluable information.

On lakes that contain wild brown trout, autumn will see a migration up the feeder river as they head for their spawning areas. Pike fully understand the rhythms of the water where they are the dominant predator. They will often assemble at the mouth of the feeder river to intercept the concentration of easy prey.

If we're lucky, there will be days when the pike themselves reveal where they are hunting, as they swirl on the surface attacking shoals of rudd. Recently, I was fishing a sizeable lough in Ireland. I was confident that I knew the general area where the pike would be, but that still left me with a lot of water to cover. Sea birds diving and picking small fish off the surface helped to narrow my search. The pike were on station below a large shoal of perch – distinctly agitated perch! My imitative fly, fished underneath the shoal, like a fish out of synch with all the others, was hit as soon as I started to retrieve it.

Even on days when there are no obvious clues as to the pikes' whereabouts, if we fish our way methodically along a likely looking contour, there is a reasonable chance that we'll connect with a fish. It's useful to keep a record of where – and just as importantly when – pike are caught. Accumulating this information will help you to improve your catch rate in the autumn. Building up this detailed local knowledge will also help you fine-tune your fishing strategy in the winter when the pikes' metabolisms have slowed down somewhat and takes are harder to come by.

As I mentioned in Chapter 1, the best way to succeed with catching pike is to get to know the rhythms of a small number of waters – perhaps a single water. However, I do enjoy adventures on new waters. Pike can be decidedly unpredictable so autumn, with its generally consistent pike fishing, is a good time to investigate new venues. My approach is simple. I try to identify areas that offer both cover and food supply. I look for water that is of medium depth – between 6 and 12 ft – and that has the right features to attract the pike. If those features include a sharp drop-off, I start to get excited. If I'm fishing an Irish lough that contains a good head of wild brown trout, I will look for the main feeder stream or river. In the autumn, the trout will run upstream to spawn. This will give the pike a restaurant, a concentration of prime calories. Also, the river will have cut a channel into the lough. There will be reed-beds along the adjacent banks, probably with died-back lilies in front of them, perhaps with a sharp drop-off with the added bonus of the remnants of ranunculus.

However, simply finding a prime location won't in itself connect you to a pike. Although autumn pike fishing is generally good, not every pike in the water will instantly launch itself at your fly. To succeed, we need to understand

▶ Pike on! Andy Bowman bends into a good Scottish fish.

how and where to fish our fly. I tend to divide autumn pike into lurkers and hunters.

In pursuit of the former, I may anchor my boat within relaxed casting range of the marginal weed cover. I will fish in both directions, casting tight into the cover and also covering the open water on the other side of the boat. To catch the lurker taking cover hard against the reed-bed, my cast will need to clip the brown stems. The lurking pike may not be prepared to move more than a foot or so to take my fly, so I will painstakingly try to cover the whole length of the reed-bed. I will probably use a slow-sinking intermediate line so that, as I retrieve towards the boat, I can fish my fly slowly and enticingly down the drop-off. The pike lurking in the deeper water away from the drop-off demands a cast away from the margins. I will then count my fly down and fish it slowly back towards the boat, close to the bottom of the water. Again, this will require a lot of casts in the arc, as the lurking pike won't be prepared to move far to hit my fly.

The hunter requires a different approach. If I fish my fly high in the water, the hunting pike, with its binocular vision and eyes set high on the head, can view it over a larger area. A pike which is hunting actively may be high in the water, so to fish a fly along the bottom may mean that it goes unnoticed. In any case, if that pike is close to the bottom, it will be quite happy to surge up in the water to grab what it perceives to be an easy meal that's worth spending some energy on – hence my preference for three-dimensional flies. If I'm fishing the same piece of water from the bank, I may well opt for a floating line, let my fly sink to the point where the front of my fly-line is being pulled under the water and then fish my fly slowly up the slope.

If I'm fishing what I regard as a prime location, I take my time. I set out to cover the whole column of water. Simply looking to cover a lot of water by drifting and working a fly fairly quickly may catch some pike – on a lucky day, it may produce several pike. But I'm greedy! I want to catch as many pike as possible; I want to catch the heavyweight, rod-bending specimen. If I catch a pike from one spot, I don't up-anchor and head off to the next location. Pike aren't shoal fish, but often several good fish will be in the same area for the same reason. In October 2002, I caught three pike over 20 lb fishing from one spot on the bank at my local estate lake (I also landed four double-figure fish). I took a particular pleasure in this as the boathouse on the lake houses a splendid photograph taken in 1884 of Alfred Jardine, the doyen of Victorian pike-fishers, resplendent in oiled leather waders, with a pile of five pike at his feet weighing more than 100 lb in total and including three fish of more than 20 lb. In November 2007, one of my guiding clients had eight double-figure fish from the boat in the same anchored position in an hour and a half – phenomenal sport. Don't get the wrong idea. Sessions such as these are exceptional, but being in too much of a hurry to fish the next spot may deny you a red-letter day that you would cherish for years to come.

In the autumn, I will often fish big, wild waters. I've already mentioned lough fishing by way of example and a large lough in Ireland or a Scottish loch can present us with an enormous volume of water in which to find the pike. We can only catch them if we're fishing in the right place. Because autumn pike are keen to feed, getting to grips with what the prey-fish are up to is a key ingredient to a successful campaign. I will confess to resorting to using a fish-finder/echo sounder to help me with this. A fish-finder isn't a fish-catcher however and we need to understand how to use the information it can provide to the best advantage.

During a recent autumn, I was fishing an Irish lough with a small group of English anglers. It was a water that had previously been kind to me but this week, we were struggling. Everyone was catching the odd pike but we weren't connecting with the sizeable beasties that I knew were present in the lough. I fired up the fish-finder and located a huge shoal of prey-fish, some fifty yards from the bank, at mid-water in an area where the lough was about 40 ft deep. My boating partner made a few casts to search out the water using a

► Andy Bowman caught this superb Scottish 30 lb pike in October. If you fish where big pike live, the autumn can often be the most productive season. Note the water-disturbing head on Andy's big perch-pattern fly.

slow-sinking line and did get a follow (albeit unenthusiastic) from a small pike. We went ashore, put the kettle on the stove and tried to activate the brain cells.

I've often read articles advising anglers to fish for pike in areas adjacent to their larder. I try to take it a stage further. I've frequently referred to the fact that pike don't feed all day every day. I aim to find 'the restaurant' and to fish it when the pike are feeding. I opted to concentrate on a reed-fringed drop-off, close to where the prey-fish shoal had been holding. My reasoning was that the shoal would come in to feed closer to the bank and that it was here, with the benefit of the cover provided by the died-back weed growth, that the pike would hunt them. At least we had a plan and were concentrating on our fishing rather than aimlessly covering the water.

The plan worked. Later that day, the hefty pike in the photograph walloped my bream-imitating fly as soon as I stated to retrieve it, after casting tight to the reed stems. The 26 lb beauty fought like only Irish pike can, making long, powerful runs that reminded me what colour backing I had on the reel. That pike had a belly full of fish. You could tell what she had been eating from the bream-shaped outlines pressing out of her stomach.

It's always gratifying when a carefully thought out plan bears fruit. Although autumn pike fishing is generally good and consistent, pike fishing is rarely straightforward. To be successful, we have get several things right. As always, the most important factor is location. However, the time of day can be important as well. On a perfect day, when the pike are well and truly 'on', they may well feed throughout the day. On a normal or more difficult day, the pike may restrict their feeding activity to quite specific time windows. Often, as with spring, these most productive autumn times will be at first light and at dusk, but each lake will be different. There will never be a substitute for detailed local knowledge and experience but you can only gain that by putting in the hours on your selected water and taking careful note of your results.

▼ Often timing is every bit as important as location. This splendid Irish pike from the 'secret lough' (Fish of the Month for November 2008) was caught by me after much plotting and scheming! It was one of the hardest-fighting pike I have ever encountered and made an extremely long run against a well-bent rod to show me the colour of my backing! It's always satisfying when a carefully thought out plan produces the desired result. (Paul Armishaw)

Sometimes, quite specific events can bring the pike on – a hatch which triggers prey-fish activity, a rise of degree or two in the water temperature, or better light levels. Sometimes it's just where the hands on your watch are pointing. If I'm not certain of the 'magic pike time' on a particular water, I pick three or four areas which I think warrant attention and fish them repeatedly, in rotation. Recently, I was guiding Jonathan Simmons on a stretch of the Upper Bristol Avon. It's a typical small, lowland, English river – beautiful and largely ignored by the coarse anglers who want more predictable fishing. The weather was vile – it was blowing a gale and the rain was trying to work its way through our supposedly waterproof clothing. During the brief gaps in the rainfall, we had managed the odd small pike but we weren't setting the river alight! It was on the third visit to a run along a reed-bank that Jonathan connected with the splendid pike in the photograph. It was the biggest pike that I had ever seen from that stretch of river and must have been covered on each of the two previous visits.

▼ Jonathan Simmons with his 'third attempt' river fish.

Apart from location and time of day, the other piece which we have to fit into the jigsaw puzzle is our choice of fly and how we present it. Here, we enter the realms of magic and mystery! The most successful fly that anyone can attach to their leader is one that they have confidence in. I'm fortunate to have caught enough pike to feel confident in my fly selection. I don't waste time by constantly changing my fly and I'm driven to distraction by guiding clients who get disheartened when they haven't connected with a pike after ten minutes and think that changing the fly will somehow send the pike into an uncontrollable feeding frenzy.

In the autumn, my objective is to put my fly in front of a feeding pike. My choice of fly is governed by two considerations – available prey-fish and water clarity. If the water is reasonably clear, I opt for my basic three-dimensional streamer, tied to suggest the predominant prey species. If the water is coloured, I put my faith in the ubiquitous yellow and orange streamer. Normally, this unadventurous approach is all that is needed; the pike takes, the rod is bent and all is well with the world. Inevitably, there are times when the cantankerous pike don't co-operate, times when I know I'm covering fish but can't get a response. When I'm convinced that this is the problem, I modify my approach. Rather than try to trigger the pike's feeding response, I'll try to provoke it.

These inexplicably difficult days may see me rigging a fly that I would normally reserve for slow, winter fishing. The extra wriggle that I can impart with a double bunny may just get me a result. Strangely, a fly which works when all

◄ The flies are chosen. It's time to hunt the hunters. *(Gardiner Mitchell)*

else fails isn't a better fly on a better day. I will confess that I don't really understand this. Perhaps a pike that has a full belly and isn't inclined to feed can be stimulated by a fly with an exaggerated action. Perhaps that same fly just doesn't move through the water in a way that gives off the appropriate signals to a pike that is hammering a shoal of roach.

I'll also try some less natural colour combinations. Pink works for Rod Tye, the renowned guide on Lough Mask in Ireland. Whilst I personally don't feel right using a pink fly for pike (it's too pretty!) I'll happily tweak a fly tied in colours that bear no relationship to any fish in the water. I was persuaded to try this after several sessions when someone fishing a stretch of water after me caught pike on an outlandish creation – pike that I knew I had previously covered. This reinforces an essential point for any pike fly-fisher. Never think you know all the answers. Always be willing to learn something new. Remember, the pike haven't read this book and are perpetually willing to puzzle us!

Autumn can face us with difficult fishing conditions. In particular, heavy rainfall may put more colour in the water than is ideal. This problem is especially prevalent on waters fed by streams that are liable to flood and, of course, on rivers. Pike are efficient, highly developed predators that aren't reliant solely on their excellent eyesight. However, as I've stated before, pike don't eat every day and if conditions aren't ideal for hunting they may opt to wait until circumstances are more favourable. Nevertheless, there are practical limits to this. As mentioned earlier, my local estate lake is fed by a stream which floods during periods of heavy rain. This results in suspended silt being washed into the main body of the lake. To describe the water as coloured would be a distinct understatement – opaque would be a better term! Sometimes, if the pike were to wait for a dramatic improvement in visibility, they would get hungry. On such occasions, I have had some success with the rattler. I say 'some success' guardedly. This hi-viz, noisy fly has helped me catch some hefty autumn pike in conditions that conventional wisdom would have decreed were totally unsuitable for fly-fishing. However, like the excessive action of the double bunny, the noise produced by the rattle tied to its under-body only serves to get the fly noticed. It doesn't work miracles. If the water is reasonably clear, the rattler is often best left in your tackle room.

When I embark on my autumn pike-fishing campaign, I aim to gather as much knowledge and information as possible about the water I have elected to fish. This means that, early on, I will fish some long sessions, from dawn to dusk. As well as identifying good locations to hunt pike, I try to ascertain the 'magic pike times' for the water. These special times, when your chances of a take are markedly better than others, vary from water to water. There is no substitute for local knowledge based on experience. Because autumn pike fishing is so good I tend to cram in as much personal fishing as possible, along with my busy guiding schedule. These personal fishing sessions are usually shorter affairs – after all, I have other, more mundane tasks to attend to. By accumulating as much data as possible, I can get the maximum benefit from my fishing efforts.

Often, these shorter sessions involve bank fishing rather than taking out a boat. If you are fishing from the bank, your ability to cast a long line can be crucial. If there are pike swirling, attacking prey-fish along the drop-off twenty-five yards or so from where you are standing, it can be desperately frustrating if you can only cast fifteen yards. Sometimes the answer is to use a smaller fly – say 4 or 5 in. A smaller fly, even if less appealing, will be more effective than a larger fly that simply isn't covering the pike. However, the real answer is to bring your casting up to the highest possible level. If your technique is letting you down, enlist some help from a good instructor. (Make sure that the instructor you choose realises the size of the flies you are using. Methods that can whiz a trout fly towards the horizon can be rather less useful when dealing with full-bore pike flies.) Study the mechanics, watch videos, practise in the park. It will take effort and perseverance but if the reward is a 20 lb pike, caught at a distance you couldn't manage before, it will be supremely satisfying and worth all the hard work. Don't ever try to increase your casting distance by turning the process into extreme cardiovascular exercise. Brute force doesn't outperform a good, relaxed style. I will often fish many days in succession in the autumn. If I had a ragged casting technique that involved too much physical effort, I would soon be in trouble, exhausted and suffering from wear and tear to my joints. As it is, I have every intention of continuing my pike fly-fishing into my dotage.

Fine-tuning your tackle will also influence your ability to cast long distances. I've previously referred to the need for balanced tackle. This isn't just important for comfort and relaxed fishing, it's also crucial if you want to stretch your casting performance. Often, when I'm not too bothered about casting range, I'll simply fit a level leader to my fly-line. When I'm aiming for maximum distance, I'll take the trouble to construct a tapered leader. (You can also buy knotless tapered leaders in suitable breaking strains.) I may also use a shorter leader than normal – perhaps as short as 4 ft. There are times when an extra few yards can be more relevant than presentation. Don't misunderstand me. I don't think that being a hot-shot caster makes anyone a good fly-fisher. I avoid turning my fishing sessions into tournament casting exercises. However, to be a good pike fly-fisher, able to get the best results from your fishing efforts, does demand that you master the problem of casting big flies. You need to learn to double-haul effectively. Since this is a practical undertaking, I can't teach you how to achieve with in the pages of this book: you will have to address it as a separate issue. However, time and effort spent on improving your casting technique will give you enormous pleasure and satisfaction and will add to your enjoyment every time you venture onto the bank.

Sheer distance aside, autumn can present us with another casting problem. It is the season when we're most likely to be confronted by an awkward wind. If you are right-handed, the most difficult breeze is one which blows from right to left (even worse if it's slightly into your face). This tends to push your fly and your line across you and can make casting big pike flies decidedly hazardous. When casting trout flies, I simply switch to casting backhand, over my left shoulder. However, this technique doesn't work with pike flies as I can't generate enough line-speed to be in proper control of my cast. I therefore developed what I thought was a revolutionary answer. I cast backwards, aiming my cast behind me (benefiting from a favourable wind direction) and delivered my back cast at the water. Of course, I've since discovered that, far from being revolutionary, this technique had been used by good casters for many years. It even has a name – 'the Galway cast'.

The other dreaded wind is the one which blows strongly into your face. You can combat this by changing the position of your casting arc. Rather than the forward cast being at ten o'clock and the back cast at one o'clock, you can tilt your arc forward to between nine and twelve o'clock. The back cast is then tossed high and benefits from the breeze, whilst the forward cast is driven under the wind. The same technique can be used in reverse if you have a strong wind blowing from behind.

Autumn is a fabulous time to fly-fish for pike. They will often feed well, as if conscious that the hard times of winter are in the offing. If we are lucky, then the weather will be kind – cool perhaps, but not so cold as to be uncomfortable for us or to slow the pike down. There are still enough hours of daylight to give us plenty of fishing opportunities. If there is good cloud cover, the pike may well be catchable throughout the day. Inevitably, there will be some rain. If we are lucky, it will come in small doses – enough to freshen the water but not torrential rain that floods the rivers or renders the lakes opaque.

The countryside can be spectacularly beautiful. My local old estate lake looks stunning, the surrounding woodland a mass of browns, oranges and amber, shot through with the evergreen colours. The Wye Valley is a picture-postcard delight. It's as if nature is putting on a brave and defiant show, prior to being shrouded in the greys of winter.

If you are an all-round fly-fisher, who spends the spring and summer in pursuit of trout and salmon, autumn pike can extend your fishing season. Like me, you may well come to enjoy your pike fishing so much that they will become your principal quarry for the whole of the year. I treasure the opportunity to fish for pike in the autumn. It provides markedly better fishing than the summer and gives me the motivation to continue my efforts through the winter.

▲ Autumn can produce some fabulous colours to add a magical dimension to our fishing. This Scottish loch is putting on a fine show before the hard, grey days of winter. *(Andy Bowman)*

Chapter 9

WINTER TACTICS

AUTUMN IS INEVITABLY followed by winter. The last leaves fall from the trees and the countryside is laid bare and grey. The days get shorter, the nights longer and the water temperature drops. The pike slow down and we have to refine our tactics.

I'm often asked the question: 'At what temperature do pike stop feeding?' The honest answer is that as long as the water is liquid, there is a chance of tempting a pike. I have caught pike when most of the lake has been covered in ice. My walk to the bank has been marked by King Wenceslas-type footprints in the frost. My warm breath has hung in the air like smoke from my pipe. After two or three casts, I have had to scrunch the ice from my rod rings. But pike are a northern fish and will still be catchable in water temperatures that render other species completely inactive.

The actual temperature is, in fact, less of an issue than the direction in which it is moving. A sudden, sharp drop in temperature gives us poor prospects. If it stays cold, the pike will adjust – they will get hungry and feed. A steady rise in temperature will see our prospects improve and if it stays mild and settled, there is every chance that we will enjoy some good sport.

Sometimes, the Weather Gods relent and we get spells of mild, settled conditions even in the middle of winter. Grey cloud cover keeps the night temperature from dropping much below the daytime levels and the water loses its bitter edge. At such times, the tactics which caught us pike in the autumn will continue to be successful. The same hotspots will yield up pike and all will be well with the world.

To be honest, though, I wouldn't recommend starting a campaign on an unknown water in the middle of winter. You are more likely to have success if you fish a venue with which you are familiar. Knowledge gained in the autumn, when the fishing was easier, can prove an enormous help in the winter. This knowledge can allow us to target our efforts both in terms of location and time. Whilst in winter, the pike will still be catchable, they won't feed as often or as vigorously as they did in the autumn. In the autumn, when you see a pike swirl as it hits a shoal of prey-fish, if you cast into the middle of the ensuing ripples, you will almost certainly be rewarded with a good, solid take as the pike hits your fly. Cast into that same ripple in the middle of January and you could be disappointed to discover that the pike has eaten its fill.

Generally, we can expect to get fewer takes in the winter. This means that we should lower our expectations but ensure that we concentrate hard on our fishing. Although we're unlikely to catch as many pike as in the autumn, the average size can be high. Big pike seem to have less of a problem with chilly conditions than do their smaller relatives. If you only get one take in the day and land a 20 lb pike, you will head for home enveloped in a warm glow of satisfaction. If, however, you make a hash of that one take because you have slipped into 'mechanical fishing', then you will head for home in a lather of frustration.

When the day is cold and the fishing is slow, it can be difficult to maintain your concentration. I try to combat this problem by making a point of taking breaks during the session. My tackle bag will contain a flask of kick-start coffee that I brewed in the morning. By the time I pour it into my mug, it will have achieved a consistency and a bitterness that definitely jolt the brain back into action. I also go through the arcane ritual of filling my pipe with strong tobacco and struggling to light a match with numb fingers.

If slow fishing can dull your senses and your reactions, it's equally difficult to maintain your concentration when you are cold, wet or uncomfortable. If you are going to fly-fish during the winter, you need to sort out your wardrobe. The insulated boiler suit option favoured by some coarse fishermen when fishing for pike in the winter doesn't fit the bill for fly-fishing. Nowadays, we are well served with clothing designed for fly-fishing which is weatherproof and breathable. The old wax-cotton jacket may have kept the weather out, but it also kept the sweat in. The result was a clammy, chilling layer of clothing next to the skin. Layering up with underwear that wicks moisture away and insu-lating fleece under an outer shell of breathable Gore-Tex means that we can keep our bodies warm without hampering our ability to cast. Clothing aimed at the shooting fraternity is robust and also serves us well. My wife and teen-age daughter berate my lack of fashion sense. I don't care. Technical Tweed breeks, Polartec long johns, breathable wading jackets and shooting jackets may not set the catwalk alight but they prevent winter fly-fishing for pike from becoming a masochistic pursuit.

If the main body is easily looked after, the extremities give us more difficult problems. I have failed to find gloves that keep my hands warm but allow me to retain the 'feel' I want when I'm fly-fishing. Bare hands, retrieving fly-line, get spattered with drops of icy water which act as an efficient heat-exchanger system. The pain can be excruciating. The fly-line cuts into your fingers: fishing ceases to be a pleasure. Whilst I haven't found gloves to solve the problem, my wife – a nurse – has found me a solution. There is a substance, marketed as Aqueous Cream, which, when worked into the hands prior to fishing, offers a good degree of protection from the cold. There is, however, an altogether better solution. The adrenalin surge generated by landing a good pike works wonders. Somehow, your frozen hands are shot through with warmth, the pain is a distant memory and you regain full use of your fingers.

If cold hands are unpleasant, cold feet can rob us of the will to live. Again, we need to balance insulation with ease of movement. Moon boots may keep your feet warm if you are fishing from a chair but you wouldn't want to walk very far in them. Ordinary rubber wellies may keep water out, but they also keep sweat in, so can be horribly cold when you aren't hiking along the bank. Apart from my wading brogues, I rely on two sets of footwear. The first is a pair of lightweight, breathable, waterproof hiking boots. They are great for boat fishing or anywhere that I don't have to slosh through too much water or mud. The second is a splendid pair of leather wellington boots, aimed at the shooting fraternity. They are waterproof, breathable and ideal for striding over rough, muddy banks.

If you are dressed to withstand the rigours of the winter weather, then you can put your mind to the important task of catching pike.

I've already referred to the fact that pike feed less often in the winter than in spring or autumn, and this means that I will try to target my efforts to ensure that I am fishing at 'magic pike time'. On some waters, this will be the same as in the autumn. On some waters, at some times, midday – when the water temperature is at its highest – can be a key time to fish.

The fact that the pike will feed less often also has a bearing on my choice of fly. If a pike is only going to make one hit in the course of the day, I want that one hit to be on my fly. To achieve this, I want my fly to look as if it's worth the pike expending precious energy on. Why should a pike chase four 2 oz roach, if there is one 8 oz roach on offer? This means that I'll often attach a larger fly to my trace. A 9 in streamer tied on a 6/0 hook demands good casting technique. My first effort with a really big fly was a few years ago and my casting ability was somewhat limited. Despite not being able to cast my fly more than fifteen yards I did catch a couple of good pike. This was a couple more than I had been catching on previous sessions and encouraged me to persevere with improving my casting skills. Winter will also see me using flies with more movement. I want to present the pike with something irresistible; something too tempting to be allowed to escape. My winter fly-box will contain double bunnies, tied in both imitative patterns and hi-viz, yellow and orange dressings.

During the winter, because I'll often be using large flies, my 10 weight rod will see more action than my 9 weight. Because I'll often be fishing deeper water, my reel will normally be loaded with a slow-sinking, intermediate line. I will look to present my fly as slowly as possible, imparting an erratic jerky movement. I want to suggest an easy meal to trigger a feeding response in the pike. This can work well on the good days, on the days when the pike are willing to hunt.

Sometimes in the winter, we are faced with hard, cold conditions which can make the pike difficult to tempt. Even worse is a sudden, noticeable drop in temperature. This can find the pike ensconced in deeper water, glued to the bed of the lake and unwilling to chase our fly. Whilst these conditions are far from ideal, there is a method which can help us to scratch out the odd pike.

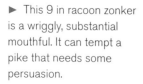

► This 9 in racoon zonker is a wriggly, substantial mouthful. It can tempt a pike that needs some persuasion.

These are days for painstaking fishing with the bomber. At the end of November 2007, Andy Bowman came down from Scotland for a few days guided fishing on my local old estate lake. He had picked his dates after careful consideration of the weather forecast. We were promised a spell of mild, settled weather with a gentle breeze and extensive cloud cover – perfect conditions, which would let us use autumn tactics and fish with confidence. I had picked Andy up from Bristol Airport and delivered him to his B&B near the lake. Everything looked set for some productive sport.

When I collected Andy at the crack of dawn the following morning, the sky was cloudless and there wasn't a hint of breeze to ruffle the mist covering the lake. The temperature had dropped from 10 °C the previous afternoon, down to minus 6 °C. The weather man had got it spectacularly wrong. We were faced with a picture-postcard scene of white frost and the lake was mirror-calm. It looked stunningly beautiful but didn't fill us with confidence! We had a few desultory casts from the bank with our 3d streamers but we both knew that the drop-off we had been planning to fish wasn't going to be productive. After wrapping our hands around mugs of hot coffee, we headed for the boathouse. We had changed from intermediate lines to high-density fast sinkers (8 in per second). Our conventional streamers had been replaced by buoyant bomber flies. The plan was simple. We were going to fish the deepest part of the lake, about 20 ft, where I was confident that some good pike would be in residence. Knowing where the pike would be was one matter – getting one to take a fly could be another matter altogether! At least rowing the boat put some warmth back into my bones.

With feigned confidence, I said that we would get a fish at 11.00 a.m. This had been 'magic pike time' on the lake and I also reasoned that the air temperature would have risen to coincide with the water temperature, so that the temperature of the lake would no longer be falling. We fished at anchor, each of us taking half of the circle around the boat. We were using short leaders. The high-density lines sank our flies and tethered them a few feet above the bed of the lake. A twitchy retrieve made the fly dive; a pause allowed it to flutter upwards enticingly. We fished slowly, making a lot of casts to cover the water methodically. The first two anchorings didn't produce a sniff of a fish. I poured coffee and lit my pipe. On the third anchoring, at 10.55 a.m., my line 'got heavy'. I knew there were no underwater obstructions to snag my fly. I tightened and felt the solid resistance of a big pike. I connected firmly and concentrated on getting my sunken line up in the water to give me direct contact with the fish. Although I could tell it was a big pike, the fight was far from lively – until, that

▲ A sudden, unexpected drop in temperature didn't make Andy Bowman or I feel optimistic. At least rowing the boat warmed my bones and took us to the deeper water where there was a chance of finding a good fish.
(Andy Bowman)

▶ The bomber, fished deep and slow, worked. I had to strip my sunken line quickly to get into 'straight line' contact with the pike. Initially, the fight was slow and lethargic. When she came close to the boat, she woke up and decided to show me just how strong she was.
(Andy Bowman)

◄ The big pike, neatly hooked in the scissors, and ready for Andy Bowman to unhook in the water. She had taken the bomber – a buoyant fly – deep in the water. It's always satisfying when a well thought out plan produces the desired result. *(Andy Bowman)*

is, she spotted the boat. At that point, she switched into overdrive and powered off on an unstoppable run. Eventually I was able to bring her alongside the boat. Andy removed the big barbless single hook, which was lodged in the scissors, without removing the pike from the water. He reached over and supported her for a few minutes until she kicked strongly and swam back into the depths. He gave me a generous handshake and berated me for my inaccurate time-keeping.

Fishing a bomber isn't the most exciting or entertaining method of fly-fishing for pike. However, it's a useful technique when you are faced with cold conditions and pike that aren't willing to chase your fly high in the water. Often the pike caught in this way will have leeches on them – a sure sign that they have been skulking on the bottom of the lake.

Scratching out a good pike was satisfying, but had we been faced with the same problem on a larger, unfamiliar water, we would probably have failed to get a take. Cold conditions that push pike into deeper parts of the lake can make it difficult to locate fish when faced with a large expanse of apparently featureless water. Big loughs in Ireland or big lochs in Scotland take a lot of work to understand. Trying to find the proverbial needle in the haystack can be a thankless task. If you look for smaller haystacks, you can significantly improve your chances of success.

Again, in the example of my local lake, had we been restricted to bank fishing, we would not have been able to cover a pike. The few season ticket holders fishing the club water, without access to a boat, all blanked on that day.

▲ Only a little one, but this pike was caught from my local river when the temperature was sub-zero and the stillwaters were all 'stiff on top'. *(Tim Westcott)*

Sometimes when you are faced with a difficult problem, rather than struggle to solve it, a better option can be to look for a venue that doesn't present the same problem. Sometimes in the winter, if the temperatures are bouncing around and I don't feel confident about finding pike in a lake, I'll switch my attentions to a river.

The Bristol Avon, the Upper Thames or the River Wye can do a lot to repair my morale. At least I know that I can cover the pike. Even the cruellest of days still gives me a reasonable chance of a fish or two. River pike need to feed more frequently than their lake-dwelling cousins simply to replace the energy expended on keeping station in the current. A bent and bucking rod can restore my sense of self-belief and rekindle my enthusiasm. The same applies to all waters where you know you can cover the pike. The Fens, some canals and gravel pits can all offer some easier fishing when the going gets tough.

Whilst fly-fishing for pike in the depths of winter can be demanding, it can also be rewarding. I may not have many monster hauls to brag about but most sessions do produce a pike or two. Often enough, these pike will be big enough to justify the effort spent on luring them. Overall, my winter fishing is more successful than my summer fishing and I certainly wouldn't neglect it.

I have talked about the problems experienced when there is a sharp drop in temperature but, alternatively, sometimes, we can get lucky. Sometimes we have the perfect day that follows a mild night. The sun shines and the temperature climbs above 10 °C. This can encourage pike into shallow areas where the water warms more quickly. It's surprising how rapidly pike can react to this slight, local rise in water temperature. You can find a small, shallow bay where there are several pike willing to hit your fly. Such days don't occur very often but they are too good to miss. Four or five good pike in quick succession can make winter seem far less daunting.

At some point, there will be a fundamental change in the winter pike fishing. Winter's grip will be less severe. The days will get longer and the water temperature will creep up. A whole new factor will start to influence the pikes' behaviour. Food supply and comfort with suddenly be of less importance than the urge to reproduce. I'm assuming that by now, you have got to know your water. The same shallow bays and adjacent drop-offs that produced such good

◄ You may get fewer takes in the winter but the pike are often sizeable. Tim Westcott was happy to be warmed up by this splendid pike (just 1 oz short of 36 lb) from an old estate lake.

sport in the post-spawn period now demand our attention. It's usually the smaller, male pike that show up first; the big girls come later.

On 1 March 2003, I was fishing with my young son – then a mere 8 years old. I had tackled him up with a spinning rod and a plug. I made my way to the piece of bank that I was planning to fish from but, before I could cast my fly, I heard a high pitched shout: 'Daddy I've got one!' I picked up the net and landed a lively pike for Sebastian. The fish was released and I walked back towards my rod. I didn't get that far before another cry told me that Sebastian was connected to another pike. He caught eight pike in an hour and a half. I didn't get to wet a line but was relegated to ghillie, just landing and unhooking his fish. I remember the session very well. Obviously I was delighted for my son but slightly peeved – after all, it was my birthday! I took note of where Sebastian had caught his fish. When I returned the following morning, I fished the adjacent drop-off. Instead of the smaller lively males, I landed a heavyweight, 24 lb female.

The pre-spawn period that is heralded by winter losing its grip is one of the three prime times to catch pike. Now the pike are keen to feed – they want to pack on calories, prior to the rigours of spawning. The change in the pikes' behaviour is, in my experience, driven more by water temperature than by the calendar. This can result in marked regional variations. Even on neighbouring waters, the pike may run to noticeably different schedules. As always, experience and observation are the keys to success.

The pike know their way around. They will follow defined routes on their way to the areas where they will get together for their nuptials. If you know your water, you can target these motorways and enjoy some fantastic sport. Typically, these routes will be along deeper channels or steep drop-offs that lead to the favoured spawning areas. In previous pages, I've made frequent reference to the fact that it's important to get to know the water you are fishing. This can be particularly significant at pre-spawn time. The actual spawning areas can be simple to identify but the routes leading to them require detailed local knowledge to establish. The pike angler who has spent time plotting the water and studying the pikes' behaviour will consistently achieve better results than the newcomer or the angler who hasn't put in the hours.

Pre-spawn pike offer us significant advantages over midwinter pike. It's easier to establish their location and they are more inclined to feed. A floating line will be the first choice as pike move in to shallower water. Basic 3d streamers will again be the most effective flies. At this time, I normally scale back to 6 in flies. These are big enough to be interesting without being too difficult to cast. You may well have some brisk sport with a veritable herd of smaller, male

pike. (Males rarely exceed 10 lb.) If you are enjoying this sport, you have two options. You can smile and keep catching the males or you can try to find the larger, following females.

Bear in mind that pike are at their heaviest now. Exercising this choice could well result in you connecting with your biggest-ever pike. There is also a chance of catching several big fish in the same session. If you land a big pike, don't make the mistake of assuming that you have exhausted the potential of an area. My usual advice to guiding clients who have banked a good fish is to get a fly back into the same piece of water immediately. Often enough, there will be more than one good fish in the same spot. I once had a guiding client shout that he had seen the pike I had hooked. He was certain it was an absolute monster. I was puzzled as I had felt the fish and although I was confident it was a good one, I thought that to describe it as a monster was probably an exaggeration. All was made clear as I brought my fish, a nice double-figure pike, to the net. A much bigger fish was swimming alongside – it was this second fish that my client had spotted. Several of my guiding clients and I have enjoyed multiple

▲ At some point, winter loosens its grip. The water temperature rises and the pike move to shallower water prior to their nuptials. This bay is also a prime spot to target post-spawn pike in the spring.
(Andy Bowman)

► Further evidence that temperature is more of a determining factor than the calendar. Mike Duxbury tempted this beauty with a huge tandem fly on March 13th. We had expected to be fishing for pre-spawn pike but unusually low temperatures meant that they were running behind schedule and we were fishing for winter pike.

catches of good pike from the same spot. Even if you don't connect with another good fish straight away, it's always worth a return visit after half an hour or so. That other big pike may have been disturbed by you catching the first fish, but may well prove catchable if you give the water a short rest.

The pre-spawn period for the pike is also courtship time for other residents of the lake. The great-crested grebes lay on an entertaining show as they perform their elaborate, ritual dances and display their smart, metallic bronze ruffs. I'm always encouraged to see them, as I have many memories of monster pike caught on days when the grebes have been showing off.

Whilst a high percentage of my midwinter pike fishing is carried out from a boat, most of my pre-spawn fishing is done from the bank or by wading the margins. This makes it easier for me to enjoy short sessions. The longer hours of daylight offer the chance of squeezing in a couple of hours at first light or dusk. It's also easier to be stealthy when fishing from the bank.

With respect to this mention of pre-spawn pike, I would emphasise here that I'm talking of the period leading up to spawning – I'm not advocating fishing for pike which are just about to spawn. That is quite simply bad practice.

I don't need a specimen pike so badly that I would fish when the big females are dribbling eggs and should be left in peace. When this stage is imminent on a particular water, I call a halt to proceedings. I take note of where the big girls are likely to be for the post-spawn fishing and enjoy the anticipation.

This close season (either statutory or self-imposed) is when I enjoy some trout fishing. This can be a pleasure in itself. It can also give me the opportunity to carry out some research on a water I intend to target for pike when they have recovered from spawning. I have trout-fished for many years. I do appreciate that, for many fly-fishers, they are a fascinating and rewarding quarry. For me, they just don't have the same appeal as pike and are strictly a stopgap as I control my impatience before I can return to pike fishing.

Chapter 10

STILLWATERS

FIRST LET ME EXPLAIN what I mean by the term 'stillwater'. In using this term, I am referring to the smaller lakes, some natural, but many the result of man's activities. These latter include gravel pits and old estate lakes, both of which can provide us with first-class pike fly-fishing. By this term, and in this chapter, I am excluding the much larger waters such as the bigger Irish loughs and Scottish lochs and the English and Welsh trout reservoirs. These waters, some of them huge in comparison to the small lakes, can require fundamentally different approaches, as we'll see in due course.

Let's look at estate lakes first. Most were created as part of the process of landscaping the grounds of stately homes. The aristocracy wanted to look out over beautiful, sheltered lakes, often bounded by splendid specimen trees. Frequently, these lakes are sited where the rolling parkland meets the wild wood. We should be eternally grateful to Capability Brown for providing us with some excellent pike fishing.

Although originally 'manufactured', many of these lakes were formed around three hundred years ago and now feel as if they have always been part of the countryside. Usually, they were created by damming a stream or a small river and allowing the valley behind the wall to flood. These lakes have a feeder stream (or streams) and an outlet stream which means that their size remains constant. Extreme flood conditions simply result in a larger throughput of water. Nevertheless, they can be heavily affected by rainfall, which floods the feeder streams and washes suspended silt into the lake. This can lead to heavily coloured, sometimes almost opaque water.

Normally, they are deeper at the dam end, with shallower areas at the top of the lake, by the feeder stream. Any bays in these areas are where the pike will come to spawn. The old stream bed may remain as a deeper channel through the lake. Where they still exist, these channels can prove useful spots to target. However, on many lakes with a silt bottom, this feature will have disappeared.

These days, estate lakes are usually left unmanaged. Various coarse fish species find their own way into the lake over the years and a state of equilibrium develops in which prey and predators thrive alongside one another. Since the lakes are usually shallow over much of their area, they are extremely fertile, packed with invertebrates which nourish the prey-fish, who in turn give the pike a nourishing diet. The best estate lakes are veritable pike factories, and home to large shoals of bream, tench, roach, rudd, perch and carp – which can pose a problem as their activity can result in suspended silt which colours the water. The pleasure anglers at my local estate lake regularly take huge catches of bream and tench during the summer months before they switch their attentions to pike fishing in the autumn and winter.

In addition to being rich in food items, these old, established lakes will be rich in features. Reeds and lilies will provide cover as well as a food supply for the prey-fish. There will be drop-offs – defined, if undramatic – along with shelves and corners which help us to locate the pike.

Gravel pits are a more recent feature of the landscape. They are the result of extracting materials for the construction industry and are particularly common along river valleys in south-east England, such as the Thames, Loddon, Darenth, Lea and Colne. Some can have more features than a cursory glance around the surface in the winter would reveal. The way that they are dug can mean that they have some interesting bars and islands – both above the water and submerged. Other gravel pits, however, are just excavated, bowl-shaped waters. These usually drop away quite steeply from the shore, which can make the margin the most important feature on the pit. Although they can shelve away rapidly, they are rarely deep. It can be worth spending some time during the close season, casting a weight and counting it down to plot the depths in different parts of the pit. If I'm faced with an apparently featureless gravel pit, I may opt to fish the north-eastern corner of the water as it's likely to be the warmest spot. Some gravel pits have murky water because they have been recently worked (or still are worked). However, many offer perfectly clear

◄ Mike Duxbury landed this superb pike, two days after opening day, on an old estate lake. It was part of a spectacular haul that we enjoyed. Mike had a pike 'drop off' which we both thought would have set a new English record. It destroyed his 11 weight rod and left him feeling distraught. I had every sympathy with him as I had lost what was probably the same fish in March that year from exactly the same spot. Mike was desperately unlucky as the hook had come adrift. I had lost the monster through rank poor fishing – I had struck too soon because I had been so shocked by the size of the pike.

water. These latter pits, often fed by underground springs, can be useful to know about. When my local estate lake is coloured to an almost opaque condition, a gravel pit can give me the chance to fish for pike that can see my fly.

Some gravel pits have been established long enough for nature to have taken over and disguise the fact that they were man-made. Some are rather less appealing, bounded by roads and feeling a little too close to human activity for my taste. That said, even these less scenic waters often contain some good pike.

It must be mentioned that some gravel pits aren't best suited to fly-fishing, having restricted banks that don't allow you to cast effectively. As always, it's worth carrying out some research before committing to a season permit.

Smaller stillwaters can be subjected to more angling pressure than makes for good pike fishing. In particular, fisheries that stay open all year and can be fished on a day-ticket basis can result in their pike population not being at all co-operative. Pike that experience too much attention from anglers can opt to spend their time well away from the banks and beyond realistic casting range. They can also become night-time feeders. Thus it's worth taking the trouble to find a water that isn't hammered by a large number of anglers (especially bearing in mind that coarse fishermen often use three rods when pike fishing.) A water that is controlled by a small syndicate or a club with restricted membership is a better proposition. If the small membership is largely made up of anglers who fish for bream, tench and carp, so much the better.

I was fortunate in that, when I started to fly-fish for pike, I had access to an estate lake that offered superb pike fishing. I was also familiar with the water, having fished it with my salmon spinning rod for several years. The estate has always kept to the English close season (15 March to 15 June inclusive). The membership of the fishing club is restricted and not all of the members fish for pike. Furthermore, the club only has the right to fish from the bank and only has access to about a quarter of the bank. This last point is very significant: the pike always have a refuge, away from the attentions of the anglers. I will confess that I have found this frustrating in the past. There have been occasions when I have known that all the pike have been in deeper water at the wrong end of the lake! But, whilst this may have been frustrating, it has also preserved the lake as a venue that produces large pike, year in, year out.

It also meant that, in my early days of fly-fishing for pike, I wasn't faced with too many problems to address at the same time. In the course of a fishing session, I could have a few casts from most of the available bank. I fished with

▼ Halfway up my rod! I caught this heavyweight pike during the opening week at an old estate lake. She was one of five pike over 20 lb caught by myself and guiding clients that week. The fact that the estate adheres to the close season and that most of the lake is 'out of bounds' means that the pike have some refuge from the attentions of anglers. This has allowed the lake to produce fabulous pike, year after year. More pressured waters may produce the occasional flurry of good fish but the quality of the pike fishing will, inevitably, deteriorate quickly.

a floating line and worked out how to get my slow-sinking fly to explore the whole column of water. I learned that when the pike were hunting actively, a fly presented high in the water would be more appealing than one fished deep. If pike were there, I had the chance to catch them. I developed flies that were consistently successful at catching pike. I learned how to impart the enticing action to my fly. I learned the importance of being observant and discovered the significance of 'fish-traps'.

On one memorable November morning, I paid a visit to the lake and elected to fish the short stretch of bank that let me cast my fly into deeper water (10 ft or so). This involved a fairly strenuous walk through a couple of fields. There were gates to climb over and a stream to paddle through. I was happy to be travelling light and spared a sympathetic thought for the coarse fishers who would negotiate the rough, soggy ground, encumbered by about 100 lb of equipment and bait.

The length of bank I had chosen was about two hundred yards long, with wooden fishing stages projecting through the reeds, giving me access to the water. I made a long cast from the first stage. I knew that my fly was beyond the drop-off and I allowed it to sink before retrieving it up the slope. Two or three short, jerky strips were enough. I felt a sharp jag on the line and tightened into a powerful pike. I unhooked the good double-figure fish by reaching down into the water from the stage. I felt brimful of confidence. A good pike caught immediately convinced me that my plan was the right one. A fishless hour later, my confidence was starting to flag. Maybe I had just been lucky and had put my fly on the nose of a stray pike. I hitched my hook into the keeper-ring on my rod and started to walk back towards my car.

I was puzzled. All my instincts were shouting at me that it should have been an eventful day. As I strolled along the bank, I was looking out over the surface of the lake, willing a pike to swirl and rekindle my enthusiasm. There were no tell-tale scatterings of small fish. No gulls were dive-bombing the water to snatch fry in their beaks. I left the main body of the lake behind me and walked up the bank of the feeder stream. There is a tree-lined pool at the top of the stream, where the water comes over a weir. The coarse fishers normally walk past this pool without a second glance on their way to fish the 'proper' lake. A pike swirled, causing a spray of prey-fish to leap out of the water in a panic. Then another pike swirled, then another. I was supposed to be heading for home but this was too good to walk away from.

To put a fly into the pool, I had to cant my rod over and make a flat side cast that fired my line under the trees. First cast, tighten, wham! A thumping take from a lively double-figure pike. I took four sizeable fish in five casts. The last pike turned my only remaining wire trace into a curly, kinked affair that certainly couldn't be trusted to land another fish. I was late and scurried back towards my car, high on adrenalin. I drove home with my brain buzzing. How many pike were in the pool? Later that evening, I visited a fly-fishing friend and scrounged the last foot of his Armor Pro Leader.

I was back beside the pool at first light the following morning. This short session was even better – seven good pike topped by a fish of more than 20 lb. I stopped fishing. I didn't need another pike and thought that if I curtailed my enthusiasm, I might be able to revisit the pool on another day and catch again. I had discovered why there were so many big pike in such a small area. The pool was stuffed with miniature perch – grown on from the tiny fry that had hatched in the spring. They were crammed in so densely that I had impaled a couple when retrieving my fly through the water. The weir meant that they were unable to flee upstream. The pike meant that they were unable to escape downstream.

I had an entertaining accomplice. A kingfisher was enjoying the rich pickings. It was able to take the perch off the surface, where they had been driven by the pike below. By casting my fly to the spot where the kingfisher had dived, I was able to tempt the pike underneath. This was my first-ever experience of pike and a fish-trap. I resolved to exercise some self-restraint and just catch the occasional pike from the hot-spot over the next couple of weeks. I was sure that if I fished it too often, I would spook the pike and drive them elsewhere. I caught thirty more pike from the pool before November drew to a close. I realise that some of these were probably repeat captures but I know that most were only caught once. These pike had negotiated a two hundred yard long, narrow, canal-like stretch of water, no more than 18 in deep, to reach the pool.

I fully expected that the pike would leave for deeper water when the frosts tightened their grip. They didn't. I revisited the pool many times throughout the winter and caught another two (different) pike of more than 20 lb. I caught pike when the main body of the lake was frozen. I caught pike in the eddies when the feeder stream was in flood. It was exciting fishing of the highest quality.

The reason why there was such a good concentration of sizeable pike in such a small area was the huge number of fingerling perch that were penned in the pool. Whilst large pike would normally eat bigger fish than those little perch, there were so many prey-fish that the pike were gobbling them ten at a

time. I had always been surprised that the lake didn't have a larger population of perch. I think I had discovered the reason!

I learned a great deal from this whole experience. It brought home to me that detailed local knowledge and careful observation are more valuable than mere theories. It also demonstrated that pike don't always behave as we expect them to.

I am often asked the question: 'Where will the pike be today?' I used to give careful consideration to the prevailing conditions and give a lengthy, apparently expert reply. I now know that the best answer is, 'Wherever they want to be.' Pike, especially big pike, are the dominant species in the lake. The biggest pike are tyrants and have no need to conform to any rules. I have stopped regarding the behaviour of small pike (less than 3 lb) as a guide to where the more interesting pike will be. The small fish will often stay very close to the cover afforded by reed-beds. On a good water, they are as much prey as predator. Whilst the majority of big pike that I have caught have been in the vicinity of some sort of cover, most of them have taken my fly in the adjoining open water. The old tales about pike lurking in cover to ambush their unsuspecting victims don't tell the whole story. A big pike doesn't need to hide from a shoal

▲ Smaller stillwaters are more susceptible to changes in temperature than large ones. This unexpected hard frost offered poor fishing prospects for the day. This characteristic can also work to our advantage. The same smaller water will respond more quickly to a rise in temperature than will a large, deep water.

of bream. It is too fast and too powerful to have to rely on secrecy to catch its prey. If you are catching small pike in open water, it's unlikely that your next take will be from a heavyweight specimen.

The old estate lake was the perfect venue for me to develop my pike fly-fishing skills. If you can identify a lake with similar qualities in your locality, I would heartily recommend that you take out a season's membership. If you can catch some pike, you will hone your techniques and will gain that all-important characteristic – confidence. Confidence gained on such a lake will stand you in good stead when you venture on to larger waters.

For any stillwater to produce consistently good pike fishing, there needs to be a balance between prey and predator. A useful rule of thumb is that the mass of pike in the lake will be 10 per cent of the mass of their food. How the population of pike is constituted will vary from one water to another. Some lakes will produce a large number of small pike: others will produce fewer but heavier pike. A determining factor will be the tendency of pike to predate on their own species. The best limiting device on the numbers of small pike is a hungry great grandma! The better lakes will produce the odd small pike, some fish of around 8 or 9 lb, a reasonable number of double-figure fish and an occasional 20 lb pike. The very best lakes will produce 20 lb fish on a fairly regular basis and will offer the chance of a 30 lb pike. For a lake to provide good pike fishing on a regular and consistent basis, it needs to contain enough pike to give a degree of stability as to how the pike population is made up. This means that very small waters won't offer long-term, high-quality pike fishing. That said, I'm frequently surprised by clients catching a much larger pike than I had thought a water capable of producing.

Many anglers who specialise in fishing for pike on gravel pits adopt a policy of plunder, then move on to the next water. They find an under-exploited lake and succeed in catching a number of good pike. Their success can be short-lived but they accept this and are quickly planning a campaign on another venue. Personally, I prefer to develop a longer term relationship with a water, so tend to concentrate on lakes of at least 30 acres.

Stillwater pike fishing may form the mainstay of your sport in a year. However, because you are likely to be restricted to bank fishing, there may well be times when the pike are beyond your casting range. Rather than bemoan this, accept the fact that the pike will benefit from avoiding your attentions for parts of the year. The answer is to develop your knowledge of different types of water. When the pike in the old estate lake decamped to deeper water in the summer

◄ Many smaller stillwaters don't allow boat fishing. For much of the year this isn't a problem as the pike will hunt within casting range of the shore. When conditions mean that the pike are beyond our range, rather than get frustrated, we should respect the fact that the pike have some respite from our attentions. *(Andy Bowman)*

◄ This was the first pike of over 20 lb landed by Richard Morrish. The pike took his fly in the bay where a feeder stream entered the lake.

or when the winter was hard I turned my attentions to river fishing. Now, I catch a lot of pike, including some heavyweight fish, from much larger waters in Ireland, Scotland and Wales. I know that the confidence I built up catching pike on the old estate lake has been a tremendous help in defining my approach to fishing 'big ponds'.

Chapter 11

RIVERS

Let me say straight away that I thoroughly enjoy fly-fishing for pike on rivers. They can call for a whole range of different techniques which provide variety – the spice of life – and add pleasure to my pike hunting. I fish many rivers. They all have one thing in common – the water moves. But it doesn't move in a regular, uniform way: there are bends, slacks, eddies and shallow runs that can all influence where pike will be found at different times.

Just days before writing this, I took a guiding client to fish a stretch of the upper Bristol Avon. I took him to a spot where a reed-bank protected a sizeable pocket of slack water and the main flow of the river sped alongside. I explained that he should cast across the river, let the flow bring his line and fly to the edge of the slack and then retrieve his fly slowly past the corner of the reeds. He caught a pike with his first cast – the first pike he had ever caught. He was amazed and complimented me on my advice. In truth, it wasn't that clever a trick. The same approach had produced a pike from that spot on every one of my previous six visits. River fishing lets us take pleasure and satisfaction from exercising a degree of simple watercraft.

Rivers give us the chance of reasonable sport during conditions that can make stillwater fishing dour and difficult. Because river pike have to expend energy to cope with the moving water, they also have to replace that energy. The refuelling process means that they will often feed more consistently than their stillwater counterparts. Also, they will often look to conserve their energy by taking up residence in parts of the river where they haven't got to work too hard against the flow. Occasionally, in the summer, some pike will break the rules and will take up position in shallow runs of rippling, faster water.

I catch the majority of my river pike by fishing the 'crease' – the very edge of where the main flow and the slack or back-eddy meet. This means that I'll often spend more time studying the water than simply making a fan of casts to cover an area. I try to think of things from a pike's point of view. 'If I were a pike, where would I want to be right now?' When trying to answer this fundamental question, I take a range of factors into account. I've heard people say that there will be a pike every twenty yards or so along the river. This may be the case on relatively featureless, canal-like rivers: it's definitely not the case on most of the rivers that I fish.

The first question to address is that of food supply. This is a highly 'moveable feast'. At different times of year, the various prey-fish species will favour different parts of the river, or different specific swims. The small chub that frolic in the shallow run in the summer may prefer a deeper run in the winter. Some 'all-round' coarse fishermen accumulate valuable information by fishing for bream, roach or perch. They can then use this information to their advantage when they go pike fishing. Personally, I can't get too excited about the

▼ I'm fishing a 'junction', where a side-stream rejoins the main flow on the river Barrow in Ireland. The pocket of slack water in front of the promontory is an ideal spot for a pike to hold up in and observe what succulent treats the main flow will bring.
(Jim Hendrick)

prospect of a day's roach fishing. However, you can often get valuable pointers by talking to the coarse fishermen. Finding out about the match fishing returns can also be of great help. I fish a stretch of the Upper Thames where coarse fishing matches are held on some Saturdays. Arriving at the river at midday, just prior to the end of the competition, means that I can find out which parts of the river have produced good catches of bite-sized fish that would interest the pike. Also, when the match anglers return their catches at the end of the competition, it can spark a real interest from the pike. Lots of vulnerable fish being released into the river simultaneously can stimulate the pike into definite feeding frenzy!

The second factor is comfort. Pike, especially big pike, don't like working too hard. When they are not hunting actively, they don't want to waste precious energy and burn calories by fighting against a strong current. Therefore, I always try to find areas of slack water. Sometimes these can be easy to identify. Backwaters can be productive. A pronounced bend in the river will produce an area of quiet water on the inside of the bend (sometimes on the outside too). The angler who fishes a stretch of river regularly, throughout the year, will have an edge when it comes to identifying less obvious features.

▼ Whilst river pike aren't usually quite as large as their stillwater brethren, even small rivers can produce some surprisingly big fish. Tim Westcott looks suitably pleased with his catch.

A beautiful stretch of the upper Bristol Avon I fish has plenty of obvious 'pikey' spots. There is a section of the river, straight, with parallel banks and apparently uniform flow, that looks featureless in the winter and would be easy to ignore as you walk to the next, seemingly more attractive swim. Because I visit the river in the summer, I know that this stretch of water is more interesting below the surface than the outward appearance implies. First, I know that the far bank was a mass of lilies in the summer. In the winter, the died-back lily-bed will still provide a 'brake' on the flow of the river. Twenty feet from the bank, there is a pronounced hump in the river bed. This is obvious in the summer as it is topped by a thicket of rushes that stand clear of the water. In the winter, there is no clue to its existence on the surface of the river. I have often caught pike from this section of river. As I have stressed before, there is no substitute for detailed, local knowledge.

The third factor is cover. If a pike can be in water where it doesn't have to work too hard and isn't easily visible, it is giving itself an advantage over its prey. Again, some cover is obvious – the willow tree that has toppled into the river is there for all to see. The died-back lilies and the hump I referred to earlier also provide pike with cover. Bends will often produce undercut banks with convenient holes for pike to lie in.

If you can identify spots that fulfil these requirements of food, comfort and cover, then you are well on your way to some successful pike fishing. As with stillwater fishing, a pike's residence may be different from its restaurant. Find an ideal residence within a fin-flick of a restaurant and you will catch a pike.

Often, you will find it easier to fish these hot-spots if they are on your side of the river. This means that you will need to be stealthy. Andy Smith of the Hardy's Instructors Academy found it interesting that I fished from a kneeling position much of the time when we had a session together on the Upper Avon. Just before writing this, I spoke with him on the phone and learned that he had just caught a beautiful, 18 lb pike from the River Trent. He was fishing well back from the water's edge and knows that, had he been standing close to the water, that fish may not have taken his fly.

To fish features on the far side of the river, you need to learn how to handle your line so that you can present your fly effectively. This can be as simple as putting an upstream mend in your line. The flow in the centre of the river will generally be stronger than it is close to the far bank. The upstream bow that you put into your fly-line will straighten as your fly moves downstream, allowing you to fish close to the far bank before your fly is dragged across the current. If you are an experienced wild brown trout catcher, you may already be familiar with useful line control techniques. Learning how to handle your tackle for river fishing is all part of the challenge and adds to the pleasure.

Andy Smith and Tim Gaunt-Baker (Andy's colleague at the Hardy's Instructor Academy), along with myself, have been experimenting with using double-handed fly-rods to fish stretches of river that present problems when fished with a conventional 9 ft single-handed rod. The extra length of the two-handed salmon rod can be helpful with line control and can assist with fishing a fly effectively in some stretches where marginal weed-growth and awkward bends would make us struggle with a shorter rod. A longer rod can also allow us to cast when we have a high, steep bank behind us. However, whilst a 13 ft Spey-rod can be useful in such circumstances, I wouldn't use one as a matter of course, preferring the lightness and ease of casting with a good single-handed rod. The longer rod, contrary to popular belief, doesn't mean that you can cast further – you can't get the extra line-speed that double-hauling generates. It can also be a handicap when you are trying to cast from small gaps between trees and bushes. However, if you have got one sitting in your tackle room that only gets used for an annual expedition to the Tweed, it may be worth dusting it down more regularly.

I use a floating line for the majority of my river pike fishing. If I want to get my fly down in the water, a sinking line doesn't give me the best solution. It

◄ Andy Smith, of the Hardy's Instructors Academy, took this splendid pike using a two-handed salmon rod. The longer rod can enable you to fish stretches of river that would be difficult to tackle with a conventional, 9 ft, single-handed fly-rod.

works perfectly well for salmon fishing techniques, when fishing 'downstream and across'. However, when I'm pike fishing, I'm often trying to work my fly around eddies, in ways which require me to be able to mend my line frequently. This can be achieved better with a floating line: I often prefer to tackle the problem with a weighted fly.

In most circumstances, my first-choice fly is the ubiquitous 3d streamer. To add weight, one option is to build it into the fly's head – tungsten putty is a useful material for this. The weighted head doesn't just influence the fly's sink-rate; it also helps impart an enticing jigging action. If I'm doing a lot of river fishing, I may take the trouble to tie a selection of flies with different loadings. Another option that I use frequently is to tie a simple variation on the basic pattern by incorporating a winding of lead-substitute wire below the under-body. An alternative, flexible and practical approach is to carry a coil of such wire in your pocket. This allows you to adjust the weight of a standard fly to suit different water conditions by adding a few twists of this behind the fly's head, under the winging fibres. It can be a lot less hassle than constantly changing your fly.

Regarding fly patterns, the same basic rules apply on rivers as on stillwaters when choosing what colour combination to present to the pike. Generally, I select imitative patterns when the water is reasonably clear and the hi-viz, yellow and orange version when the river is more coloured.

I have found 'magic pike time' to be less of an issue on rivers than on still-waters. That said, certain times may well prove more productive on certain parts of a river. If I feel confident that I know where pike are in residence, I'll often revisit places that I think warrant special attention. I've often caught a pike on the third visit – a pike that hadn't been in the mood to hit my fly on the preceding attempts. As with stillwater pike fishing, it's often worth fishing at first light. Being at the riverbank before the countryside is disturbed by human activity can offer pleasures other than a bent rod and a fighting pike. A few years ago I had the privilege of sharing the water with a handsome dog otter. He seemed quite happy to go about his hunting whilst I worked my fly. I didn't begrudge him his catch!

Rivers that contain pike don't generally have banks that are neatly main-tained for the benefit of fly-fishermen. I certainly wouldn't want fishing clubs to hack down bank-side vegetation, just to make it easier for me to handle my fly-line. Wildlife needs the cover provided by the undergrowth and shouldn't be put under pressure for the convenience of fly-fishermen. If I'm engaging in 'jungle warfare', my Flexi-Stripper line tray can be helpful.

A word of caution regarding casting. Many rivers have public footpaths along their banks. Whilst these aren't quite thronged with the madding crowd, they are often popular with dog-walkers. Impaling Fido's mistress with your 4/0 hook isn't a good idea. Impaling Fido himself will probably cause even more of a problem. Furthermore, the fields adjoining the riverbank are often occupied by livestock. Lively bullocks fight very well when hooked with a pike fly-rod. If you are lucky, the worst that will happen is that your leader snaps and your barbless hook is shed by the bovine. I know of several rods that have been broken. I also know of a £20,000 bill for an (apparently minor) injury caused to a Thoroughbred racehorse. Always check that your back-cast can be performed safely. Sometimes, a curious passer-by will want to talk to you. If you are right-handed and casting conventionally, get the passer-by to stand on your left whilst you chat.

Willows and other trees lining the banks can make casting difficult. The Galway cast (casting behind you and delivering the back-cast) isn't just useful for combating an awkward breeze. It can also let you cast at a different angle and cover an eddy that you would be unable to reach with a conventional cast. I also find the ability to tilt my casting arc and cast flat and low can be helpful, allowing my back-cast to be made underneath branches that are hanging down. These flat casts do take some practice before they can be made smoothly and consistently – there is no margin for error in your timing.

Riverbanks can be steep and horribly slippery – especially after flood water has receded. When fishing places where the river flows through a steep gorge and can't be waded, I have been known to employ a device like an enormous corkscrew with a metal ring on the top, through which I can pass a rope to lower myself into a fishing position. Being careless isn't macho!

It's easy to keep a check on the condition of a local river. Every time that I drive into my local town, my route takes me over a beautiful old stone bridge which straddles the Bristol Avon. I can park my car and take a stroll along the bank. This will let me judge the state of the river and decide whether it's in good order for pike fishing. If I'm planning a trip to the river Wye – about an hour's drive from home – I have friends who live by the river who can help me out with information about the condition of the water. I don't want to make the drive and be faced with a raging torrent of old cocoa that will prove impossible to fish effectively. It makes sense to establish a network of fellow anglers who can swap such information.

I have said that the majority of my river pike fishing is carried out from the bank. I can cast all the way across most of the rivers that I fish. If you have access to both banks, even the bigger waters such as the Wye can be covered well enough. However, I do find a boat useful for fishing weirpools on the Thames. It can enable me to fish interesting pockets of water which I couldn't cover effectively from the bank. A boat also gives me access to stretches of a river where both banks are completely hedged with dense vegetation. Some very large rivers, such as the Shannon and the Barrow in Ireland, are often tackled from a boat.

To return to safety issues, weirpools and big rivers, with confusing and powerful currents, demand our utmost care and respect. A beginner is best advised to go out with a guide or an experienced angler, who knows the water well, before planning a solo trip with a boat. As always, a small, neat, fly-fisherman's lifejacket should be worn. It may sound as if I'm applying for a job as a health and safety officer but sadly, I am aware of too many people who have drowned whilst boat fishing. In Ireland, it is a legal requirement that anglers boat-fishing should wear lifejackets at all times.

Chalk streams in southern England, such as the Test and the Hampshire Avon, run clear and at a reasonably consistent level in most 'normal' weather conditions. They also hold some good pike. However, most of the rivers that we fish for pike are heavily affected by rainfall levels. The quietly meandering river, which glides through verdant pastureland, can be transformed into a swirling torrent of old cocoa after a heavy downpour. In these circumstances, fly-fishing for pike can be a somewhat pointless pursuit. However, there are occasions

▼ Weirpools are often worth investigating. They will have interesting pockets of slack water for pike to rest in and there will be prey-fish available for them.

◄ Spring-fed rivers are less susceptible to the effects of heavy rainfall and can fish well when other rivers are coloured and in flood. *(Jon Bowes)*

when we can turn bad conditions to our advantage. Sometimes when the river is running high, fast and coloured, pike will seek refuge in quite defined lies.

I know a spot on a local river where a bridge pier and a weir help create a slack area with a back-eddy in flood conditions. Bear in mind that a big pike will hold where she wants to. I have used rattlers to combat the opaque water and have had some surprisingly good results from this spot – including my biggest-ever river pike of 28 lb 12 oz. It's worth getting to know your river well. Sometimes, poor conditions will define where the biggest pike will take up residence.

I run my own river fishing efforts alongside my more serious, stillwater fishing. Although, as I've just said, big pike do inhabit small rivers, if all you want to do is catch big pike, you will probably fare better if you stick to stillwaters. However, river fishing offers us pleasure over and above the size of the pike to be caught. Often, a trip to the river and a catch of half-a-dozen pike in perfect condition, can provide a welcome, confidence-boosting diversion from fishing stillwaters in adverse conditions. Moreover, to be successful, you need to learn to handle your tackle well and to learn some watercraft. This can add a whole extra layer of satisfaction to your pike fly-fishing. Frequently, when I'm on the river, I have the countryside to myself. I'm relaxed – out for fun – a big fish is a bonus.

Chapter 12

'BIG PONDS'

I'M BIASED. FOR ME, FISHING BIG, wild waters for big, wild fish is the pinnacle of pike fly-fishing. Irish loughs, Scottish lochs and the large, natural lakes in Wales offer the chance to catch splendid pike in fabulous scenery. The Norfolk Broads may be set in less spectacular surroundings but, over the years, they have yielded up a huge number of good pike to those anglers prepared to devote time to understanding them.

Many anglers find the sheer size of these waters daunting. I regularly take guiding clients to fish on Llangorse in Wales and they think that, at 370 acres, it's a big pond. However, Lough Corrib in Ireland is 200 square kilometres, which equates to over 49,000 acres.

How do you start to tackle a water of this scale? The worry is that locating pike will be like looking for needles in a haystack. My approach is to try to identify the smaller bales of hay which contain all the needles. If you can get this right, you can find concentrations of pike and enjoy good sport. On special days, if you can get this right, you will enjoy sport at a level that will astound you.

My friend, Andy Bowman, puts a lot of time into fishing his favourite lochs in Scotland. He has had some sessions so good that it would be pointless for me to describe them – they would sound too good to be true. A dozen big, double-figure pike in an hour from Loch Awe was a recent example. I have had sessions

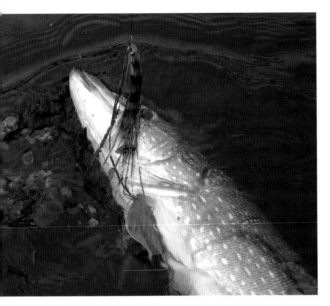

▲ Perch patterns are particularly effective on clear Scottish lochs. This superb September fish was taken by Andy Bowman on a drop-off adjacent to where the weed growth was starting to die back – autumn often comes earlier in northern latitudes. *(Andy Bowman)*

with guiding clients when I have hardly wet a line. Instead, I've been making encouraging noises as yet another pike yanks his rod into an alarming shape and I get the net ready. Don't get me wrong – sessions like this don't happen all the time, but if you work at your big-water pike fishing they will happen.

The key to success with 'big pond' fishing is simple to grasp: it's the same as with all pike fishing – 'first find your pike'. To do this, you need to accept the fact that you will have to put some effort into the process. I don't know if this volume's eagle-eyed editor will allow an expression such as 'get off your arse' to appear in print – but that is what you need to do. Find the features that will help you to find the pike.

There are charts available for many large lakes, loughs and lochs. Ordnance Survey maps can also be helpful. The information that these works contain can help you determine where to start your search. When tackling a big water, things always feel more positive if you have a plan. If you feel that your efforts are aimless, your confidence will evaporate and you will soon feel despondent. (In this respect, Tony Bennett, a pike fly-fisher from south-west Wales, recently introduced me to a useful idea. He had a contour map of a lake which, with the help of a computer wizard, had been overlaid onto an aerial photograph of the lake. The result was an easily understood illustration which made pinpointing areas quite simple.)

I look for inlet streams and rivers. They are often the scene of fish migrations and spawning activity and can be magnets for big pike. Sometimes, heavy rainfall will cause these streams to flood and they will push heavily coloured water into the lake. Although the pike may find this murky water unattractive, the 'mud line', where this silty water meets the clearer water of the lake, will often be a productive spot. Drop-offs will define pikes' travelling routes and provide them with cover. Islands, including submerged ones, will be bordered by weed growth which can house a larder for the prey-fish, which in turn attract the pike. Bays, fringed with reeds and lilies, are classic spots to target pike – particularly in the spring.

Identifying areas of the lake upon which to concentrate our efforts suddenly makes the 'big pond' seem less intimidating. Bear in mind, we are looking for feeding pike. The key factor which will determine where we fish will be the availability of food for the pike. If we can combine our knowledge of the lake's topography with an understanding of the prey-fish activity, we will be well on the way to catching pike. If we find a concentration of prey-fish and then work out where the pike will hit them, we have achieved the perfect result: we have found the pikes' restaurant. The likely location of this special place will change throughout the seasons. As ever, there is no substitute for detailed, local knowledge based on hard-earned experience.

When I venture out on an unfamiliar big water, I regard my 'fish-finder' as an invaluable tool. I use it to plot depths and contours and build up a picture of the lake's bed in an area that I have picked to survey. I'll scribble notes, sketches and diagrams on a pad. When I fish and catch a pike or two (or none!), I'll try to make sense of my results and use the information I glean to fine-tune my approach. If I'm succeeding, I will pat myself on the back, feel impossibly smug and catch another good pike. If I'm struggling, I'll scratch my head and alter what I'm doing. Too often anglers, when they are failing to catch pike, simply resolve to grit their teeth and keep going. On a big water, if you are getting it wrong, simply putting in more hours won't solve the problem.

Of course, many anglers simply won't have the time to carry out their own research. They are taking a week's holiday on the shore of a huge water they have never visited before. They know it contains some monster pike – but where? Employing the services of a professional guide can cut away much of the uncertainty. A good guide should be in touch with the local waters and understand their rhythms. If you employ a guide, listen to all forthcoming advice – it's in the guide's interest for you to be successful. (However, as a guide myself, I would make a heartfelt observation. A good guide can significantly improve your chances of catching pike. However, even the best can't guarantee that the pike will oblige. I know that taking clients out can be surprisingly stressful. I always breathe a sigh of relief when the first pike is netted.)

When you are selecting a guide, it's important that you make clear what you want to do (especially, in our context, with regard to fly-fishing). For instance, some guides in Norfolk are more concerned with maintaining 'their' score of big pike than with helping a fly-fisherman, and there are many pike-fishing guides in Ireland who prefer to troll large fish-baits or lures behind a boat. However, the best guides in Ireland have a good understanding of a fly-fisher's requirements: some are highly skilled fly-fishermen themselves. In the Appendix to this book, I have included the names, contact details and locations of a number of guides whom I know well and feel confident in recommending. I have also included a few suggested by Mark Corps of the Central Fisheries Board in Ireland. Mark is a first-class pike fly-fisher who has landed many

► Big ponds can produce big pike. I enjoyed catching this fabulous specimen from a sizeable lake in Northern Manitoba. I had some help! My guide Ernest, a Cree Indian, knew where the big pike would be. If you are visiting a large, unfamiliar water, local knowledge and expertise are invaluable.

► Another large lake in Northern Manitoba, another large pike. Ernest supports her in the water prior to her swimming off strongly.

splendid pike with his fly-rod. I have shared a boat with him on several occasions and trust his judgement in this regard.

If I, personally, hire a guide, I much prefer it if the guide fishes as well. If we try slightly different tactics, it can improve the odds of finding the best method for the day. If I am out with a client and reckon that the conditions call for imitative flies, I may opt for a perch pattern, whilst my customer uses a roach or rudd imitation. If one fly gets results, we can both fish with the catching pattern.

Some guides work on a 'nine to five' basis. Often the pike don't comply with this convenient timetable. Check with your guide as to the timing of your fishing. If I'm taking clients out in the spring, I'll often recommend being on the water at 5 a.m. – we may take a break in the middle of the day and then fish until the light goes. If I'm trying to help someone catch a good pike, I accept that we need to be fishing at the most productive times. Your guide may be prepared to be flexible but may want some extra cash for extra hours.

There is another reason for enlisting the services of a guide: good guides have worked out that drowning customers is bad for business. Some 'big ponds' will have areas that can be sensibly fished from the bank or by wading the margins (a procedure which, in some areas, is made safer by a knowledge-able presence). At certain times of year, these areas can provide productive pike fishing. However, for most of the year, a boat will be a much better proposit-ion. It will allow you to access the whole water and will enable you to cover pike without restriction. Nevertheless, if their margins require due care, the open expanses of some big waters can be decidedly dangerous places for the inexperienced. Many of the big limestone loughs in Ireland have unexpectedly rocky shallows where boats have foundered. They can also get very rough. The waves on Loughs Corrib and Mask can be whipped by strong winds until they are white horses, easily capable of swamping a boat that isn't being handled expertly. In May 2008 I was fishing Lough Key in Ireland with Andy Bowman. Our trip back to the mooring on the River Boyle was 'exciting'. I was hanging off the front of the boat to keep the nose down, whilst Andy drove us down the wind as fast as the powerful petrol engine would take us. We were staying just in front of huge waves which, had we slowed down, would have filled the boat. Andy and I have done plenty of fishing on big loughs so knew what we were doing and weren't about to panic. However, less experienced boatmen would have been in trouble. The chapter on boat fishing contains further information on boat choice and safety. For the present, if you are thinking of hiring a boat for use on a big water, or even considering buying a suitable craft, here are a few basic pointers.

1. Bear in mind that a 10 ft boat with a shallow draught that would be useful on a smaller water will often prove inadequate on a 'big pond'. A 19 ft Sheelin boat will behave much better. It will sit lower in the water and will be much less affected by the wind than will a boat with a higher prow. I have

experienced frustrating sessions with a small lightweight boat that I couldn't keep straight into the wind.

2. As with boat size/type, engine type is an issue on big waters. An electric outboard motor such as I enjoy using on smaller waters doesn't do the job on a 'big pond'. Travelling longer distances when there is a wave calls for a more powerful petrol engine. (However, I do often attach my electric motor as well as this allows me to manoeuvre my boat quietly when I am in the part of the lake that I want to fish.) Always take a set of oars with you. Rowing on a 'big pond' is hardly the first choice for locomotion but even the most reliable motor can break down sometimes.

3. 'Big ponds' are often in places that experience plenty of rainfall. If you are fishing from a boat and have travelled some distance from the mooring, you can easily get caught by an unexpected shower. Good, waterproof clothing is a must – as is somewhere to dry it overnight. Pulling on a soggy jacket at first light does little to kindle the enthusiasm for another day afloat.

4. Before venturing out, you should check the detailed, up to date weather forecast. Bear in mind that hills surrounding a 'big pond' will often generate weather conditions that are markedly different from those forecast. This applies particularly to wind strength and wind direction. If you feel uncomfortable out on the water, head for the shore – you can always go back out when the weather eases off.

Finally, I would simply urge that you accept your limitations and don't put yourself in a hazardous situation.

Assuming that you have launched your boat and armed yourself with information about attractive features, the next step is to determine the specific place to fish. If you are fishing during the post-spawn period, a useful starting point is to look for shallow, sheltered water where the pike spawn. If these shallows can be found in bays, so much the better. The principles are the same as on smaller waters – though the bays may cover several acres and need to be fished with a boat. There is no point in the pike being anywhere else. The water temperature will suit them. The shallow, weedy bays will also be playing host to the coarse fishes' nuptials. Often, the prey-fish won't be evenly distributed but will be packed into large, dense shoals. The pike don't need an invitation to the feast. They will be keen to feed and, in many instances, will have the benefit of a fish-trap to make it easy for them to manage their larder. A normal pattern of events will be that the pike hold around the mouth of the bay and at intervals head into the shallow water to feed. Usually, the most productive time to fish will be from first light until late morning when the sun is high. On some special occasions, the pike will feed throughout the day – albeit more sporadically. On many occasions, there will be another feeding period as the sun drops and the light fades into darkness.

Remember, though, that pike are unpredictable and refuse to play by the rules that we try to lay down. In spring 2007, I was fishing a perfect bay on a perfect lough. I had left my bed before daylight and was fishing my favourite bay that had produced several big pike on previous visits. Everything seemed to point to it being a successful session. The bay was full of bream and rudd and I was supremely optimistic. By 11.30 a.m. I was puzzled. The bay was obstinately devoid of the pike I had been so confident of catching. I was about to admit defeat and head back to my shore camp, when the rippled surface of the water was disturbed by half a dozen panic-stricken rudd scattering, as a huge swirl told me a pike was hunting. There were a couple more big swirls in quick succession. Now I was interested. I turned the handle on my electric outboard motor and positioned my boat so that it would drift quietly into a position from which I could cast to cover the pike. I lowered my mud anchor with extreme caution, taking care not to cause any disturbance. I felt a take on my first cast but didn't connect. A cast to exactly the same spot produced the result that I wanted. That pike weighed 28 lb 12 oz. It was the biggest pike that I caught in 2007 and a fish that I could so easily have missed.

Finding pike on 'big ponds' in the height of summer can be an altogether more difficult proposition. They will generally be in deeper water, which can mean that there are too many acres to choose from. Personally, I tend to ignore 'big ponds' in this less productive time and concentrate my efforts on different waters. This may seem a feeble, defeatist attitude, but I would defend myself by pointing out that this book is about fly-fishing for pike – it is not about insisting on fishing waters when the odds are stacked against you!

I fish 'big ponds' again in the autumn. I start by investigating the drop-offs. If I can identify drop-offs with other connected features, such as inlet streams, weed growth and islands, these places are where I will concentrate my initial efforts. I fish some waters that hold a significant population of wild brown trout. In the autumn, these trout will head for the streams, where they will spawn. This will give the pike an ideal concentration of prey-fish which they will be quick to take advantage of.

Prey-fish migration is always a factor to be aware of when fishing big waters. In Norfolk, coarse fish will move from the broads to the river systems during the winter. My favourite 'secret lough' in Ireland is connected to another (equally inaccessible) lough by a narrow channel through reeds. I have often taken a good pike from the pool where the channel opens into the second lough. The two ends of the channel act as a funnel, concentrating any prey-fish moving from one lough to the other. Pike will always be attracted to areas where their food supply has been condensed.

Winter can make 'big ponds' decidedly inhospitable. I try to pick mild spells and use information gleaned during my autumn fishing to help me to locate the pike.

Whenever you are fishing, the best approach is to concentrate on a particular area rather than trying to cover the whole water. If you limit yourself in this way, the big water will no longer feel like a huge expanse of water. Your fishing will benefit from that special ingredient that is crucial to success – confidence.

Whether or not you opt to employ a guide, it's a good idea to pick a water to which you can make return visits. As you learn the rhythms of a particular water, you will catch pike and develop a body of knowledge that will make catching good fish much less of a lottery. Don't just 'chase the news'. A report of a huge pike being caught from Loch Lomond won't help you find a similar fish when you arrive several months later. My guiding clients and I have caught a number of 20 lb pike from the 'secret lough'. You won't find any reports in the angling press which identify its location. I discovered it by recruiting local

▼ This pool, at the mouth of a channel connecting two favourite Irish loughs, is regularly home to heavyweight pike. I always take care when I'm towing the boat to be as stealthy as possible. A clumsy approach would have spooked the pike which is putting a proper bend in my rod. *(Andy Bowman)*

◀ I'm drifting the margins on an Irish lough with Xavier Lafforgue. A good boat gives you mobility and freedom to explore.
(Gardiner Mitchell)

expertise. I have learned how to catch pike there by adopting a thorough, investigative approach. There are many such waters that can reward your efforts.

My dear old dad is in his nineties. If I am lucky and have such a long and active life, there still won't be enough time to do more than scratch the surface of the gem that is big-water fishing for pike. I prefer to concentrate my efforts on a small number of waters that I feel offer the chance of good fly-fishing for pike. I would rather feel in tune with the water than flit from venue to venue.

Despite the desirability of getting to know certain waters thoroughly, one has to be practical. There are times when nothing positive can be gained from attempting to fish a particular water – and, where 'big ponds' are concerned, such efforts may be downright dangerous. For most anglers, fishing a 'big pond' involves travelling some distance. If you arrive at your destination to find that the Weather Gods have conspired to make your chosen venue unfishable, it's a good idea to have a back-up water available. Recently, I was hosting a party of English and Irish anglers. We were planning to fish my favourite 'secret lough' in County Roscommon. Unfortunately, torrential rain had caused the river which flows into the lough to flood. This river was the only route to the lough and it was impossible to get our boats in. Fortunately, our host, Kevin Lyons, knew the area very well and was able to help us launch our boats on an alternative lough. It may not have been our chosen venue but at least we were able to fish safely and we enjoyed catching some pike.

To get the best out of fly-fishing for pike on a big water, it's important to be equipped with various tackle options that allow you to tailor your approach to

► As I lifted my fly in the water, it triggered a response. This pike took the instant the fly broke the surface of the water. The technique is similar to the 'induced take' method used in trout fishing. It's a trick that has caught me many pike. It's important not to try to set the hook by striking with the rod still held high in the air. Instead, when the pike hits, I smartly drop the rod tip down to the surface of the lake, quickly retrieve the slack line with my left hand and set the hook with a firm 'strip-strike'.
(Mark Corps)

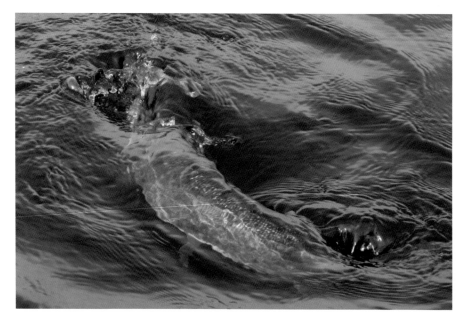

suit the prevailing circumstances. Whilst I would be happy to fish my local river with a floating line at all times, I know that this single method would be too limiting on a big water. Even during the post-spawn period, when I would expect to find pike holding in shallow water, I would still want to have a range of lines available. In May 2008 I was fishing the 'secret lough' with Andy Bowman. There had been a brief spell of warm weather at the beginning of the month and we were confident that we would find the pike responsive. However, the Weather Gods decided to amuse themselves at our expense. The wind blew from the east, the temperature plummeted and we struggled. We found pike in deeper water than we had anticipated and switched to sinking lines. We caught pike – Andy had a superb fish of 23 lb. We also found that the pikes' feeding time was much shorter and more precise than we would have expected in May. First light was by far the most productive time. The big fish in the photograph was caught in the half light before dawn.

If I'm fishing a 'big pond' at a prime time and I'm confident that I'm in the right area, I'll often fish at anchor. A stationary boat allows you to search out the whole column of water methodically. If I fail to get a quick response, I'll often pick three or four likely locations and fish them in rotation. Sometimes the only problem is where the hands on your watch are pointing; sometimes the problem is one of location. If I decide to search for hungry pike, I may well choose to drift along interesting lines and contours. I will use a drogue to slow my boat's progress and allow me to fish my fly without having to strip quickly.

I know that there are days when the pike will chase a fly that is being retrieved at speed. I also know that there are more days when a slow, erratic retrieve is more likely to entice a pike.

If you are fishing a big water and you are struggling – stop. Try to analyse what the problem is – don't just continue to plug away. If you have investigated four bays and drawn a blank, it's more than likely that the fifth bay will be equally unproductive. Try the adjacent drop-offs. Alter the depth that you are fishing. Most importantly, find the prey-fish. Often it pays to be on the water at first light. A day when it will be breezy by 9.00 a.m. can see the lake as calm as a mirror at dawn. Rudd, roach or perch will often give away their location by dimpling on the surface. If the water is flat calm this can be spotted from a considerable distance. Use your eyes. Where are the grebes and cormorants hunting? They will often help us identify the right area in which to target the pike.

Many 'big ponds' offer the chance of a truly big pike. They can be hard places to fish. They will always be challenging. Somewhere, in a huge, fertile lough there is a pike that will cause the record books to be rewritten. I'd like to catch it. Even if I don't find it, I'll enjoy trying! Success on big waters needs to be earned. Every year, I spend several weeks fishing 'big ponds'. It can be good to return to my more intimate local waters but I'm always planning my next adventure.

▲ Whilst location is the most important factor for catching big pike from big ponds, timing can also be crucial. Andy Bowman took this 23 lb specimen fishing with me on the 'secret lough' in Ireland. She hit his fly in the half-light before sunrise in late May.

Chapter 13

TROUT RESERVOIRS

I<small>N</small> E<small>NGLAND AND</small> W<small>ALES</small>, many of the reservoirs that have been stocked with trout have become productive places to fly-fish for pike. On the face of it, they are similar to many large natural lakes. However, the character of these reservoirs and the ways in which they are managed can mean that the pike don't play by the same rules as on the 'big ponds'.

Many reservoirs will let you fly-fish for pike when they are open for trout fishing. This means that during some years, we will have the opportunity to fish for the pike at all three prime times – pre-spawn, post-spawn and during the autumn. However, as these reservoirs open for fishing in March, there will be many years when we will miss out on pre-spawn fishing and will leave the pike in peace until they have recovered.

Some reservoirs, such as Chew in Somerset, have additional days when they open specifically for pike fishing. On these occasions, they allow coarse fishers to use dead fish-baits and lures. These dates are often fully subscribed in advance. Personally, I would rather give these dates a miss. Thirty boats, each with two anglers armed with two rods, is too frantic for my tastes!

The trout reservoirs are convenient places to fish. Most have a well-appointed lodge with a tackle shop and cafe facilities. They have good boats available for hire, equipped with reliable petrol engines. They can supply life-jackets and are usually manned by helpful staff who can advise you on where to

► Fat as a pig! Whilst the pike in trout reservoirs probably derive the bulk of their nourishment from the resident coarse fish, it can't be denied that they also benefit from the extra calories afforded by the stocked fish.
(Andy Bowman)

fish. The staff have a concern for your health and safety and won't let you out on the water if the weather is too rough. (Some of us hardy, macho characters, used to fishing in less-cosseted circumstances, can find this somewhat irksome at times! However, it should be remembered that these people have a duty of care for all anglers, with a wide range of boating experience and skills, and it has to be said that, in the event of any sort of emergency, there is always someone on hand to offer assistance.)

One drawback with these reservoirs is that they don't open at the crack of dawn, so often you can't start fishing until after the pike have stopped feeding in earnest. Also, several reservoirs have nature reserve areas which are out of bounds to fishermen. This can be great for the wildfowl population and I have, for instance, enjoyed watching ospreys on Eyebrook and Rutland Water. However, these restrictions can pose a problem. At post-spawn time, you can find yourself with access to a large expanse of water but all the pike can be concentrated in the area you can't fish!

Because these reservoirs exist to solve water supply problems, they can be subject to considerable variations in water level. This can mean that sequences of events which can be predicted on natural waters simply don't happen. The classic, weedy shallow area where the pike would spawn could be a dry mudflat at spawning time. Weed-beds which might provide cover for prey-fish are sometimes cut back to make fishing easier for the trout anglers. By their very nature, reservoirs will usually have fewer features than loughs or lochs and pike can therefore prove much more difficult to find.

The pikes' behaviour can also be influenced by random events. At regular intervals, some kindly soul releases lots of plump, juicy rainbow trout into the water. Although the pike will generally be more inclined to predate on the coarse fish in the reservoir, they can't be expected to ignore this bonus. This can cause a degree of conflict with the trout fishers who are convinced that the fearsome pike will diminish the trout population. In fact, I suspect that many of the trout eaten by the pike are fish that have been caught and released and weren't faring too well.

For the reasons given, I find it much harder to predict where pike will be at any given time on a reservoir than when I am fishing a natural water. Therefore, I will often adopt different tactics. Whereas I would often fish at anchor on a lough, I will be more inclined to fish on the drift when tackling a reservoir. I will normally rig my drogue to slow my boat's progress, but I will stay mobile. This, in turn, can mean that the spool housing my favourite floating line will remain in my reel-case. Instead, my first-choice line will normally be a slow-sinking

◄ Andy Bowman with a 25 lb porker from Chew. This was just one (and not the biggest) of several big pike that took his own drab perch pattern on the day. Andy described it as 'sensational fishing'. I made a point of tying some similar flies for myself that evening before returning to the water the following morning, when we again enjoyed excellent sport.

FLY-FISHING FOR PIKE

intermediate and I will also have faster-sinking lines to hand. However, I don't want to imply that I just drift around aimlessly for the day. I make good use of my fish-finder and will look to cover contours that I feel might be productive. When I catch a pike, I make sure that I repeat the drift. I also try to establish some co-ordinates on the shore that will enable me to return to the catching spot – this is important. If the waves are pushing the boat along briskly, it is all too easy to lose track of precisely where you were when the pike hit. If a particular spot proves productive, I may well opt to lower the anchor quietly and concentrate on that area for a while.

When I am fishing a reservoir on the drift, I am prone to suffer from a dangerous malaise. If I'm not connecting with pike and am just searching the water I tend to lose that feeling of anticipation that keeps the senses and reactions sharp. A few years ago, I was fishing at Chew on a bitterly cold, rain-lashed day in March. Neither my guiding client nor I had felt a pike and the day was dragging. We were close to admitting defeat and heading back to the jetty when I had a savage take that nearly dislocated my shoulder. Instead of calmly connecting with what was obviously a good pike, I clammed up and my leader was snapped like a strand of cotton. I cursed my incompetence and set up the boat to cover the same piece of water. I had another take. This time I performed slightly better and a powerful pike surged away putting a full bend in my rod. It came adrift after about thirty seconds. I cursed again, more loudly than before. Two more drifts over the same water failed to elicit a response. I realised that I had probably missed out on a fish or a pair of fish that would have turned a failure into a session to remember. Fortunately, this story has a happy ending. We fished an adjacent bay for about twenty minutes and then returned to where we had found the good pike. This time, I was prepared. I felt the take. I didn't overreact but confidently stripped and struck and connected firmly to a 20 lb pike. On a less fortunate day, my lack of concentration would have meant a frustrating, blank session.

Because the water in the trout reservoirs is usually destined for our household taps, it is usually reasonably clear. This means that my first-choice flies will be imitative patterns. (I will also have some trusty yellow and orange flies available for when the water is more coloured.) I tie a few 3d streamers to suggest rainbow trout and they usually produce a pike or two. If the fishing is slow for no discernible reason, I may resort to a large double bunny. I think that there are times when reservoir pike are too full of rainbow trout to be inclined to feed. On such days we need to trigger a response rather than find a hungry pike.

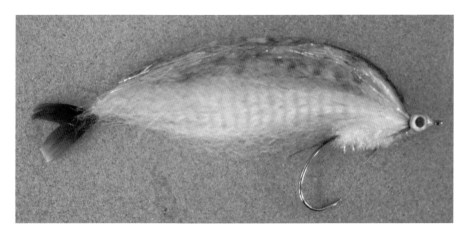

▲ This fly, tied to suggest a stockie rainbow, was produced to goad some pike-hating trout fishers. It worked – it also caught plenty of pike! The feather tail is supported by a length of classical guitar string (3rd G). I think, as fly-fishers all, we should be tolerant. After all, whilst it must be admitted that that pike do eat stockie rainbows, the revenue provided by pike anglers also funds the production of lots more stockie rainbows!

◄ Even when the fishing is 'sensational' we still need to keep our strength up. A break, some good food and some brain-jolting fresh coffee can keep you fishing at full concentration for the rest of the day. (*Andy Bowman*)

If you want to fish on my favourite old estate lake, you will need to join a waiting list and wait until a membership becomes available. You will need to buy a permit for the whole season. The trout reservoirs are available to all and can be fished on either a day-ticket or a season ticket basis. (Nevertheless, if you wanted to concentrate on one reservoir and intended to fish it many times in the course of a year, it would prove quite costly once boat hire is included.) However, these reservoirs do give us the opportunity to fish waters that we know contain huge pike. At the time of writing, the current, official British pike record came from Llandegfedd in Wales and I'm sure that several other reservoirs have the potential to produce truly monstrous pike. The introduction of stockie rainbow trout has a bearing on this as the pike have the benefit of additional nutritious food at regular intervals.

► Tim Westcott with a 20 lb, post-spawn pike from Chew. This pike was caught in late May when other waters in the area were shut for the coarse fishing close season. Pike spawn earlier than the coarse fish and this specimen was fully recovered and tested Tim's tackle to the full.

I make no secret of the fact that I prefer to fish wild natural waters. I find it a somewhat sanitised experience when I visit a reservoir. However, I'll spend a few days every year fishing for pike on these waters. A day trip to Chew, Eyebrook or Rutland can be a more realistic proposition than an expedition to Loch Awe. Reservoirs can also allow me to fish in reasonably clear water on days when my local rivers are in flood and the old estate lake looks like cold cocoa.

◀ Martha Thomson proved that you don't need to be a strapping, macho hulk to fly-fish for pike. Her relaxed, double-haul technique meant that she was able to cast big hairy pike flies a good distance. We enjoyed watching the osprey at Eyebrook as it dived and caught a pike.

I think that every pike fly-fisher who doesn't live close to a magnificent natural water should spend a few days on a trout reservoir every year. Some of these days will inevitably be unproductive but this can be easier to bear if you have already caught a good number of pike from a river or a kinder stillwater. The reservoir may prove difficult to master but it offers many fly-fishermen the chance of landing their biggest pike. It can also, on a special day, produce a veritable haul of big fish that would be hard to match on a small stillwater.

Chapter 14

BOATS AND BELLY-BOATS

Much of my pike fly-fishing is carried out from a boat. Rather than say 'a boat', perhaps I should say 'various boats'. I have my own boat and I also make do with whatever I can hire on some waters. I know some people who own several boats and have them moored on various waters in different countries. I think I would struggle to justify that sort of financial outlay to my long-suffering wife.

Fishing from a boat

If you are new to boat fishing, it's likely that your first ventures afloat will involve using a craft that is available for hire at a particular venue. Such boats will vary from the ideal to the frankly appalling. I fish a beautiful lake in Wales. The boats there may be suitable for a summer picnic in glorious weather, but when it's blowing hard, they are difficult to handle. You need to have the upper-body strength of an alpha male mountain gorilla if you are going to row one. Their design features innumerable projections, clearly intended to trap your fly-line. The seats torture your buttocks. There are no anchors and the first job of the day is to bale water out of the bottom of the boat. (To be fair, they do float.)

Rowing can be pleasant enough exercise on a balmy day, if you are not intending to travel too far. On a rough day, it can leave you feeling as if you have gone fifteen rounds with Mike Tyson. The following day can be dramatically foreshortened by you not getting out of bed until mid-afternoon! I have accumulated various items of equipment which I can use to make a boat more suited to my needs, the first being a motor.

▶ Andy Bowman has fine-tuned his boat to ensure that it doesn't have projections to grab his fly-line. The electric outboard motor is ideal for positioning the boat with the least possible disturbance. *(Andy Bowman)*

I have both a sweet, electric outboard and a more powerful petrol engine. The electric motor is perfect for smaller lakes (up to about 300 acres). It is quiet, smooth and easy to manage. It allows me to position my boat very precisely without disturbing the pike. It's powered by a deep-cycle, marine battery. These come in various capacities. My preference is for an 85 amp hour battery (often, I'll take a pair, as a single one can struggle to last all day on some waters). A bigger, 110 amp hour battery is twice as heavy. If it has to be carried any distance, it can be a nuisance. The advantage of the extra capacity can also be nullified if you are fishing for several days in succession, as it can take too long to recharge. If you get home after a long day afloat and find that when you need to depart in the morning, your battery is only three-quarters charged, you are lugging extra weight around with no corresponding benefit.

The petrol engine doesn't run out of charge and has the extra power needed when there is a wave on a bigger water. Sometimes, I'll fit both motors to a boat, using the petrol engine for the travelling and the electric for stealthy positioning of the boat in the area that I am fishing.

I have a few different types of anchor. I make my own mud anchors by filling a largish plastic flower pot with concrete and embedding a ring spanner so that I can attach a rope. These are fine for silty bottoms. I also have a traditional, pointed anchor. A word about anchor ropes – make certain that they are strong and in good condition. I once witnessed an incident that looked like a scene from an old, slapstick comedy film. Someone was fishing near me and managed to get his anchor stuck on the bottom of the lake. He stood up to pull on the rope with all of his considerable strength. The rotten rope snapped and he toppled overboard with a mighty splash. Fortunately, he was wearing a life-jacket and the water wasn't too cold. It was an embarrassing way for him to cut short his fishing session.

Use an anchor that is suited to the nature of the bottom of the lake that you are fishing. Have a lot more rope available than is needed merely to reach the bottom. An anchor will hold much better if it is on a longer rope at a shallow angle. Also, ensure that your anchor will actually stop the boat from drifting. A length of heavy steel chain between the rope and the anchor itself can help with this. Always be careful about how you lower the anchor (and insist that your

▲ The boat is set up with a petrol motor for travelling long distances, and a stealthy electric engine for positioning the boat and setting up drifts.
(*Andy Bowman*)

boat partner is equally considerate). Dumping a weight overboard with a splash will make your stealthy approach irrelevant. Clattering a chain down the side of the boat will alert every pike in the vicinity. I have experienced 'the boat partner from hell' – the person who can't keep their feet still and lumbers around in the boat like an epileptic hippopotamus. It doesn't contribute to a successful fishing session.

Sometimes I find it useful to use two anchors. I may want to orientate the boat in a particular line relative to a feature such as a reed-bank. To achieve this, I will anchor both the front and back of the boat – or 'fore and aft' as we old sea-dogs say. The technique is simple. Point the front of the boat into the wave in line with how you want it to lie. Lower the front anchor and reverse the boat, maintaining the line, whilst paying out more rope than needed. Carefully lower the anchor at the back of the boat. Using the spare rope, gently pull the boat back towards the front anchor. At the same time, let out additional rope at the back so that you don't dislodge the rear anchor. This should hold the boat nicely parallel to where you want to cast.

A swivelling boat-seat can make a day afloat a more comfortable experience. I have one with a supporting back that I can strap to the thwart in the boat.

Many boats that are provided for hire have slatted duckboards in the bottom to help keep the crew's feet dry. These snag your fly-line with frustrating frequency. It's aggravating to have the perfect cast pulled up short because your line is tangled. A simple plastic sheet in the bottom of the boat can solve this problem. Rather than slatted duckboards, my own boat is fitted with shaped plywood sheets with small holes in. They are every bit as effective and don't catch the line.

The boot of my Land Rover contains a simple, homemade baler. I used my filleting knife to modify a 6-pint plastic milk container.

An echo sounder or fish-finder is a useful piece of equipment that can save you a huge amount of time when visiting a new, large water. I used to fit the transducer to the hull of the boat with the rubber suction cap that was supplied with the unit, until I discovered that many boats have a paint finish which means that the transducer falls off at regular intervals. I have since made a device with a short, adjustable post and a G-clamp which allows me to mount my fish-finder on the gunwale of most boats. I know that some purists regard the use of such modern technology as cheating. However, in itself, a fish-finder won't catch pike for you. What it will do is give you the water temperature and a picture of the bottom of the lake. This is invaluable information which will help you to determine the best areas to target. You can get this information with a thermometer and a plumb-line but it will take a lot longer. If you have booked a weekend to fish a large, unfamiliar water, it helps to maximise your fishing time. It can also help you to locate shoals of prey-fish. You then need to be able to use this information to improve your chances of catching pike.

The bottom of a boat isn't the best surface on which to unhook a pike. I always take a large unhooking mat with me, which is laid out ready in the bottom of the boat. In most cases, I try to unhook pike in the water and support the fish before it swims off. Whilst this is achievable on most occasions, there are times when a more deeply hooked pike needs to come aboard.

If I intend to fish from a drifting boat and there is a wave, I take a drogue with me. This is like a parachute in the water which acts as a brake on the boat's progress. If a pike is hooked, it's always a good idea to pull the drogue aboard to avoid it becoming entangled with your fly-line.

Casting from a boat is an altogether different experience from casting with solid earth under your feet. If you are planning a first trip, it is worth practising beforehand. I recommend to guiding clients that they take a chair out into the park. It may draw some amused comments from passers-by but it is better than struggling when you are actually fishing. Remember that your fly-rod is an extension of your forearm. Anyone afloat who insists on pivoting their upper body when casting will rock the boat and send a series of shockwaves through the water, which will spook the pike. If you are guilty of this, you will make an annoying boat partner. If your boat partner behaves in this way it will spoil your fishing and seriously reduce your chances of success. It's always best to position your boat to allow for relaxed casting that doesn't disturb the water. If you are fishing with another angler in the boat, under no circumstances should either of you try to turn it into a casting competition.

If you are new to boat fishing, take the trouble to learn how to handle a boat. Go out with a professional guide or an experienced boat angler. Understand how to prime and start a petrol engine. Watch someone with a good rowing technique. When you are travelling with a wave on the water, try to head into or along the wave. Taking your boat across the wave can make it unstable. On a rough day, try to use the shelter afforded by an island to tack across the wind. Don't ever go out in a boat in conditions that might cause you problems. Always wear a life-jacket. Even the strongest swimmer will be beaten by cold water and layers of constricting clothing. It may seem boring and tedious for me to labour these points but inexperienced, foolhardy anglers drown every year.

▶ I am out on Lough Key in Ireland with Andy Bowman. Big, wild waters like this can be dangerous places. This was a rough day – not a time for inexperienced anglers to take chances. The boat was a proper craft, the engine was powerful and reliable and we were both competent to deal with the conditions. Every year, anglers get into trouble by venturing out in conditions that are beyond their capabilities. If you intend to fish big ponds, learn how to handle a boat, keep a close eye on the weather and don't take risks. *(Andy Bowman)*

Thoughts on boat ownership

If you decide that you want to buy your own boat, there are a number of factors to bear in mind when making your selection.

• Where are you going to fish?

• How are you going to transport the boat?

• Where are you going to store it?

A small flat-bottomed punt may be fine on a small, sheltered lake on a balmy summer's day. It isn't suitable for a big Irish lough when the wind is blowing and the surface of the water is angry. A little boat can be fun and useful if you don't expect too much of it. My personal choice is a lough-style boat. To sensibly accommodate two fly-fishermen, it wants to be at least 14 ft long: mine is 16 ft. A 19 ft long Sheelin is perfect, but the extra length makes it more of a problem to store, transport and launch. These boats are relatively narrow and sit quite low in the water. A boat with high sides gets blown about in a strong wind and is much harder to handle. A little boat isn't necessarily easier for solo use. When you sit in the stern to control the motor, the prow sticks up out of the water and any breeze can make it difficult to steer the boat in a controlled way.

You may be able to moor your boat on the water you intend to fish with it. This is an obvious solution to the problems of transport and storage but doesn't help when you want to fish another venue. To do this, you will need a trailer. A proper boat trailer is more than a platform for towing a boat. It will also help you to launch your vessel either via a convenient slipway or by reversing it into the lake. A manual winch and rollers will help to get the boat on and off the trailer. If you are looking to buy a second-hand boat, try to find one that comes complete with a compatible trailer.

A sizeable boat with a trailer demands a vehicle that is capable of towing it without too much strain (and acquisition of such a set-up may also require checking licence categories and insurance cover). I also take my boat to some remote spots without convenient road access. A four-wheel drive vehicle with genuine off-road capabilities is an essential piece of equipment for me. During 2008, Ireland experienced unusually heavy rainfall. The trip to my 'secret lough' involved covering some very difficult country. My Freelander sank up to its axles and the party had to make a 'bog road' with brushwood before we could get back to a firm tarmac surface.

▼ Although I caught this Welsh pike within casting range of the shore, I wouldn't have been able to cover it without a boat. The dense reed beds made bank fishing impractical but the boat allowed me to fish, casting my fly along the drop-off.
(Paul Armishaw)

Whether you commission a splendid new boat from a specialist builder or buy one cheaply second-hand, you can incorporate some features to make it more useful for your fishing. Every boat is host to gremlins who are intent on wrapping your fly-line around anything that gets in the way. Lockers under the seats can encourage you to stow the contents of the boat away neatly. An outboard, manual winch for lifting and lowering the anchor can help you to do it more stealthily. It also means that you don't have untidy piles of anchor rope in the bottom of the boat. You can build in your fish-finder and house its screen in a waterproof protective cover. My friend Andy Bowman has gone to much trouble to ensure that his boat has no internal projections or line-snags. I have learned that attention to detail in this regard makes for a much more enjoyable day.

If you have decided that you must have a boat, don't rush into it. Picking the right boat for fly-fishing is every bit as important as picking the right rod or reel. It's worth putting some hours into fishing from various boats before committing to buy one. The right boat will feel like a good old friend. My young son Sebastian is always pleased to learn that a fishing trip together will involve taking the boat. Somehow, it feels like more of an adventure.

Belly-boats

A few years ago, belly-boats (also known as float tubes) came on to the scene. Many greeted them with hoots of derision, dismissing them as too bizarre for serious consideration. The early versions were made from an old lorry tyre inner-tube with a fabric seat slung across the middle. More modern, sophisticated versions are a U-shape. The angler sits supported by the fabric seat with the tube wrapped around the midriff. You stay dry by wearing chest waders. Propulsion is by means of flippers attached to the feet. Proper, scuba divers' flippers are much better than the shorter ones which are often supplied with the belly-boat. Getting in and out of the water with one of these can look rather comical and can provide anyone watching with much entertainment. Trying to walk whilst wearing flippers is potentially hazardous – walking backwards can be safer!

Despite this, I have got one: I love it. Mine has five internal bladders which should make it unsinkable. It has useful, waterproof storage pockets on the arms which can house lunch, a fly-box and the few items of tackle I need for a fishing session. My first experiences with my belly-boat saw me fishing remote hill lochs for wild brown trout. These were waters that could only be reached

◀ My belly-boat lets me fish water that I couldn't cover from the bank. Here, I'm casting a popper at the emerging lilies on a favourite Irish lough. The belly-boat is an affordable, convenient and easily transported alternative to a conventional boat. Fishing from a belly-boat is a strangely relaxing experience. You feel at one with the water and can get surprisingly close to the fish without spooking them. *(Andy Bowman)*

by trekking cross-country. I suppose that I could have flown in by helicopter but that would have been too extreme. I carried my partially inflated belly-boat, strapped to my back. Take note – the belly-boat's straps are for transporting it, not for tying yourself in. I thoroughly enjoyed this wilderness fishing experience and decided to try the craft on some pike waters.

Paddling gently along a lily fringed drop-off on a gentle day is a wonderfully relaxing experience. I would find it hard to explain why but when I'm out in my belly-boat, time seems to move at a different speed altogether. The world turns more slowly and I feel part of the lake. I have seen all manner of fish swim around my flippers – apparently oblivious to my presence.

A belly-boat puts limits on the distance you can cast a big pike fly. You are low on the water – even more so than when fishing from a conventional boat. I like to use a rod with a progressive action that loads quickly and lets me cast with the absolute minimum of effort. The 'body pivot' style of casting is completely useless. It just causes the belly-boat to swirl around and delivers very little energy into your cast. Fortunately, long-range casting isn't necessary. A stealthy approach will allow you to get very close to the pike without spooking them.

The first fish that I caught from a belly-boat were feisty wild brown trout of little more than 1 lb in weight. I brought them to hand and unhooked them in the water without any problem. The first big pike that I hooked was a different kettle of fish. It powered away, heading for the sanctuary of the lilies. I bent my rod, applied plenty of side-strain and stripped back line to try to turn it. What actually happened was rather different from what I had intended. Instead of me bringing the pike safely towards me, I was pulled towards the pike. The pike made it into the lilies and slipped the barbless hook. I ended up looking confused, embarrassed and fishless in the middle of the lilies. An angler fishing from a boat took a series of photographs of the episode which he took quite sadistic delight in showing me afterwards. He laughed so much, I was worried that he would have a seizure. I resolved to improve my technique. Now, when I connect with a sizeable pike, I paddle with my flippers to maintain my position whilst playing the fish. I intend to take my belly-boat to my favourite 'secret lough' soon. I am looking forward to experiencing the Irish equivalent of a Nantucket sleigh ride.

It's important that you are confident about 'chinning' a pike if you fish from a belly-boat. You need to hold the fish firmly under the jaw, lift its head out of the water and remove your fly. I always have a set of long-nosed pliers attached to a D-ring on the right arm of my belly-boat.

▶ David Dinsmore, the editor of *Irish Angler* magazine, with a splendid pike caught from his belly-boat. My first encounter with a sizeable pike from a belly-boat proved somewhat embarrassing – I hadn't realised how far a good fish could tow me and finished up in the middle of a lily bed!

Belly-boats are a pleasure to use in calm conditions. I wouldn't advise taking one out on a 'big pond' when it's blowing hard. Flipper power is fine when you don't have to battle against a strong wave but it has its limitations. I'm also less inclined to use one when it's cold. I have ventured out in neoprene chest waders, with layers of fleece underneath, but the cold does eventually penetrate.

▲ This Irish beauty had a belly so full of fish that I could see their shapes pushing through her skin. *(Paul Armishaw)*

To be honest, I find fishing from a 'proper' boat more effective. However, a belly-boat can open up some fishing that you simply can't get to with a boat and trailer. It can also be convenient for a quick session. They are best stored partially inflated. A few puffs at the water's edge and your belly-boat is ready to go. A word of warning – don't put a fully inflated belly-boat in your car. On a sunny day, the heat generated by the light shining through the windows can make the bladders expand with disastrous results.

Being able to fish on, rather than just beside, the water, opens up areas that would otherwise be inaccessible. I regard my boat and my belly-boat as invaluable help-mates in my pursuit of pike.

Chapter 15

DESTINATION FISHING

I N THESE DAYS OF EASY, (relatively!) affordable travel, there are many of us who have come to regard fly-fishing for pike as an international sport. I count amongst my friends anglers from America, Canada, Sweden, Norway, Denmark, Holland, Ireland, Scotland, Wales and France. I have caught pike from many different countries. A fly that tempts an English pike will also tempt a Scottish or Swedish pike. Techniques and tactics that you have honed on your local waters will translate very well for overseas adventures. Before heading off to enjoy fly-fishing for pike in a new country, it makes sense to ensure that your casting is up to scratch. Your pleasure will be limited if you are struggling to handle your equipment. If you are planning to spend money on visiting a remote water, it may make sense to build the cost of some casting lessons into your budget.

Jetting off (or catching a ferry) to a far-flung destination doesn't guarantee you success – far from it. You will probably be spending a week trying to catch pike from an unfamiliar water. If you were doing that closer to home, you wouldn't expect instant results. If all you want to do in life is add to your list of monster pike caught, you will probably fare better by staying at home. However, there are all sorts of other reasons for visiting new countries.

That said, all of the destinations that I am going to refer to in this chapter do offer the visiting angler the chance of a truly monstrous pike. If you are planning an adventure, it is a good idea to maximise your chances of success.

I would always recommend enlisting the services of a guide. If you are paying good money for travel and accommodation, it's pointless to economise to the detriment of your fishing. If you are going as part of a group, the cost of the guide's expertise can be shared. Also, you may only require the guide's services for a day or two before you feel confident to tackle the new water. By way of example, I recently fished in Northern Manitoba. My guide for the trip was a Cree Native American by the name of Ernest. Apart from putting me on to some fabulous 'trophy' pike, he also enhanced my enjoyment of the whole experience. His knowledge of the local wildlife was considerable and he was able to show me many fascinating sights and teach me lessons that I will always treasure.

What you take with you will be determined by where you are going and what facilities exist at your destination. Some specialist fishing lodges will have good tackle available and some guides will be able to provide equipment. That said, I have a very personal relationship with my rods and reels and always like to take my own gear.

On recent trips that I have organised and hosted, I have been surprised at the incidence of rod breakages experienced by my clients. This has prompted me to take a spare rod whenever I am travelling on my own. If I am looking after a party of anglers and have travelled to the destination with my car, I will have brought a whole range of extra rods.

For several years, I have used four-piece fly-rods. Modern carbon fibre technology has enabled the top manufacturers to produce four-piece rods with smooth actions that are indistinguishable from two-piece versions. A four-piece rod will fit in your suitcase. A two-piece will incur a surcharge as 'sports equipment' from an airline and will be more vulnerable to rough handling.

A remote location is unlikely to have a well stocked fly-fishing emporium that sells your favourite brand of line, leader or wire trace material. It's best to take more kit than you expect to use. I will usually make sure that my leader and trace materials are of a heavier breaking strain than I would generally use at home. Pike in remote places can surprise you with how hard they can fight.

One particular word of warning! Take more flies than you think you will need. On a recent trip to Canada, I took thirty splendid, freshly tied examples. As I neared the end of my ten days fishing, I was pulling my last intact flies away from any small pike that were chasing them. My guide was highly amused and remarked that he'd never previously taken someone out who was trying so desperately to not catch a pike! Several hundred toothy beasties had completely shredded most of my collection.

Cheap flights are usually synonymous with meagre luggage allowances. The scales that I use to weigh specimen pike are often called into service to ensure that I don't exceed my allotted quota. You may well be faced with the problem of having to thin your luggage out. I would always sacrifice 'non-fishing' items rather than what could turn out to be an essential piece of equipment. The smart new jacket that will look stylish in the bar in the evening will probably never get worn. The wet-weather clothing could well be crucial to your enjoyment of your trip. I have been known to board an aeroplane wearing my chest waders and wading brogues. I have worn my wading jacket and looked obese. The game pocket in the back of the jacket has been stuffed with socks and thermal underwear. I don't regard setting out on a fishing expedition as a chance to display my sartorial elegance!

Whenever I organise or host a fishing trip, I supply my clients with a list of equipment that I think they will need to bring with them. Often, I will bring items myself that I know it will be difficult for the anglers to transport. This will include spare rods, reels and lines, landing nets and perhaps most important, life-jackets. (Note that airlines don't allow you to pack fly-fishing life-jackets that incorporate gas cylinders.)

If you intend to hire a boat at your destination, do some sensible research before you arrive. Ensure that it will be suitable and comes equipped with a motor, oars and an anchor. These items don't fit inside your suitcase.

Wherever you are travelling to, make sure that you will be able to dry wet fishing clothing. Pulling on soggy, cold clothes at first light doesn't get the day off to a good start. If you are taking waders, take a repair kit as well. I speak from experience. Chest waders that have sprung a leak could be used as instruments of refined torture.

If you decide that you want to cast a pike fly in a different country, meticulous planning in advance of your trip will help ensure that it is a memorable and enjoyable experience.

I will confess that I have had some wonderful adventures that have been completely spontaneous and unprepared. These have been in Ireland where it seems that everyone you meet will take time out to help you enjoy your stay – but that's another story!

In this chapter, I refer to destinations that I know about from personal experience. There is a limit to how much experience anyone can cram into a normal lifespan. I'm certain that I have neglected some countries that offer fantastic pike-fishing opportunities. For that I can only apologise and hope that the inhabitants of these unmentioned paradises will forgive me.

Ireland

Ireland is the closest a pike fly-fisherman will get to heaven whilst still breathing. It's a country with a small population and a huge amount of water. Much of this water contains pike. There is relatively little fishing pressure and no statutory close season for pike fishing. Legend has it that a pike of 92 lb was captured from Lough Derg in the late 1800s. This may sound like a 'fisherman's tale' but, having fished Lough Derg on several occasions, I wouldn't be so sure. There are many famous loughs in Ireland with an established reputation for producing big pike. There are also innumerable, little-known waters, many with enormous, untapped potential. Many of the loughs are large waters which can be dangerous places if the weather turns against you. It is always best to have an alternative, sheltered water available for times when you are being 'blown off' your first-choice venue. I have enjoyed some fabulous 'accidental' fishing on waters which no one has ever heard of.

Irish pike grow quickly. A fish may reach 20 lb by its fifth year and 30 lb by its seventh. Irish waters can be extremely fertile, supporting huge populations of coarse fish for the pike to devour and thrive on. The old pike record was a 53 lb fish from Lough Conn but, like many old records for various species, this has been thrown aside. (Many of these old records may well have been valid – i.e. correct in terms of weight – but the information surrounding their capture does not fulfil today's criteria for record claims.) The current official record of 42 lb 12 oz is highly vulnerable.

Ireland has a magical atmosphere. It is a land full of kindly, hospitable people who live life to the full and enjoy themselves at every opportunity. It's infectious. I have met many people who have returned from a fishing trip saying: 'The weather was dreadful, the fishing was mediocre – we had a fabulous time'. This is because, whatever the weather and fishing conditions, you can sample the famous black beer and enjoy the 'craic'. Listening to traditional music being played in the pub with passion and consummate skill is compulsory. Beware! Many anglers who travel to Ireland for a week's fishing get mysteriously waylaid – I speak from experience.

Tourism Ireland has worked closely with the Irish Fisheries Boards to promote pike fishing and to ensure that visiting anglers have an enjoyable time. They have produced an invaluable book – Pike Angling in Ireland – which is packed with useful information. It lists professional guides, centres of excellence, angler-friendly accommodation and boat-hire contacts. It is also possible to glean much useful information from tackle shops and even the bar

◄ The late Rod Tye was famous as a catcher of wild brown trout from Irish loughs (particularly Lough Mask). What was less well known was that Rod was also an enthusiastic and knowledgeable pike fly-fisher. I valued his help with designing flies and will miss his encouragement and advice. Rod lived on the shore of Lough Mask and caught many fine pike from this imposing water.

◄ When you are fishing far from home, a knowledgeable guide can make a huge difference to your fishing success. Xavier Lafforgue is helping me to select a fly and is discussing what tactics we should adopt for the session. *(Gardiner Mitchell)*

of a local pub. If you opt to stay in one of the many B&Bs approved by Tourism Ireland, it's worth checking that they will accommodate you regarding early starts to the day. Most will and some will provide a packed lunch for anglers who want to be on the water before the traditional cooked breakfast is served.

Spring and autumn probably offer the visiting angler the best chance of success. I also fish in Ireland during the winter because I am familiar with several wonderful loughs and have friends in the area who help me locate the pike. If you have a knowledgeable guide and time your trip to perfection, the pre-spawn period (probably from the middle of February to the middle of March) could produce a huge fish.

Fly-fishing for pike is my job, so I am able to justify the amount of time that I spend on it. Fly-fishing for pike in Ireland can be extremely addictive. Be careful! A book has been published recently with the title *Till Death or Fly Fishing Do Us Part*. I recently had a guiding client who had told his wife that he was away 'on business'. Some of the mobile phone conversations which members of the party overheard were highly complicated – don't worry, your secret is safe with us!

Recently, there has been much publicity about the damage being done to stocks of pike in Ireland by immigrants from Eastern Europe. They had been netting many waters to catch pike for the table. This problem seems to be diminishing, thanks to the efforts of the Irish Fisheries Boards. There has also been much controversy regarding the practice of culling pike to protect trout numbers. Again, this is becoming less of a problem as people are becoming better educated regarding the effects pike have on a water. In any case, Ireland continues to provide superb pike fishing. I fervently hope and expect that this will continue to be the case for the future.

Scotland

Scotland is similar to Ireland in many ways. It boasts strikingly beautiful, majestic scenery. Many of its lochs are set between impressively wild hillscapes. Its pike fishing 'industry' is rather less developed than Ireland's but there is plenty of help available for the visiting angler. The old British pike record was a fish of 47 lb from Loch Lomond. (In my opinion, while the Lough Conn 53 lb fish mentioned earlier may have been valid, I'm pretty much con-vinced by the Loch Lomond fish and would personally still be prepared to accept this as the actual record.) Loch Awe (affectionately known as Loch Awesome by many of its devotees) is famous throughout the world for the huge brown trout it produces. It is also a superb pike water. A visit to Glasgow's Kelvingrove Art Gallery can stir the enthusiasm of a pike fly-fisher. On view is the Endrick pike head – the head of a pike found during the 1300s in the river Endrick's (a tributary of Loch Lomond) marshes. The best estimate is that this pike would have weighed about 70 lb. Loch Ken in Dumfries and Galloway is also reputed to have produced a pike of more than 70 lb. Today, Ken is regarded as one of the most productive waters.

Currently, many members of the Pike Anglers Club of Great Britain rate Scotland as the best place to fish. The Pike Fly-fishing Association have recently organised some very successful events there. The big lochs such as Lomond and Awe can be every bit as wild as the large Irish loughs so the advice about having alternative fishing available is just as relevant. Whilst many anglers will choose to fish the famous lochs with a reputation for big pike, there are some huge fish lurking in waters that have yet to be fully investigated. I have enjoyed good sport on lochs that were reputed to hold no pike at all!

▼ Loch Awe in Scotland – an awesome loch that is home to awesome pike. *(Andy Bowman)*

Like Ireland, Scotland has no statutory close season for pike fishing. On average, Scotland is slightly cooler than either England or Ireland so can often 'fill in the corners' of your pike fly-fishing year. Pre-spawn and post-spawn times will commonly be about two weeks later than elsewhere in the British Isles. In 2007, I finished the season on the fourteenth of March fishing in my shirtsleeves. I was catching good pike and was frustrated that the calendar had brought my fishing to an end. A few days later, I headed north of the border with Tim Westcott. We were lucky to be staying in a delightful lodge owned by Michael Bell, the boss of Bloke Fly-rods. It was in a beautiful setting overlooking the river Ettrick, a tributary of the Tweed which is well known for its salmon fishing. We were fishing a pair of lochs in the area. Instead of shirtsleeves, we were clad in neoprene chest waders, layers of fleece and heavy wading jackets. We weren't fishing for the pre-spawn pike we had anticipated. It was winter, real winter, complete with snow blizzards and freezing temperatures. We caught the odd pike and took a perverse pleasure in trying to work out how to cast our flies into the howling wind. Tim caught his first Scottish pike and was amazed at how hard it fought. Spring can come later in Scotland and can provide first-class fishing when the pike in England are becoming dour. When stillwaters in England are 'cooked' at the end of the summer, Scotland can offer wonderful, autumnal fly-fishing for pike.

The days of Scottish game anglers regarding pike as vermin are fading fast. Many Scottish salmon fishers are waking up to the fact that pike are an exciting sporting quarry. My friend Andy Bowman is just such an angler. He has been a supremely successful salmon fisherman but now concentrates, almost exclusively, on his pike fly-fishing. His efforts have been rewarded with some superb pike, including fish of more than 30 lb. He doesn't restrict his efforts to the famous lochs and has enjoyed some wonderful sport on unknown waters.

Scotland is easy for English anglers to travel to. There is much good pike fishing south of the Great Glen. I normally drive rather than fly – it means that I can take my own boat. You can hire boats in Scotland but – away from the main centres – it can prove difficult.

Sweden

Sweden has many superb lakes and rivers which contain good pike. It also offers an opportunity to do something that surprises most anglers, namely, catch a pike from the sea. The Baltic can provide the visiting angler with some fantastic pike fly-fishing. It has relatively low salinity and the pike prey on

herring and small cod as well as the expected fresh-
water fish. Stuart Longhurst once regaled me with
a tale of a pike that contained a cod which contained
a belly full of sandeels. Herring come close to shore
to spawn in the spring. I once watched a shoal of
prey-fish swim under the boat – I think they were
bream. That shoal was the size of several football
pitches. The abundance of prey-fish in the Baltic
adds a tingle of anticipation to every cast.

To fly-fish for pike in the sea may seem a daunting prospect. This is taking 'big pond' fishing to
another level! In truth, it's much less intimidating
than you would expect. The Swedish Archipelago
contains more than thirty thousand islands. These
frame areas of water with channels in between. It's
more like fishing a series of interconnected loughs than fishing a huge, featureless expanse of water. Because there is so much water available – both on the
Baltic and inland, on rivers and lakes – the fishing pressure is relatively low.

One day, someone will catch a pike from the Baltic that will cause people to
reassess what it takes for a pike to be considered big. In June 2008, I had the
pleasure of fishing with Johan Broman, a well-known Swedish fly-rod designer
and expert Baltic pike-fisher. His boat was unlike anything I had previously
used for pike fly-fishing. Its 115 horsepower engine gave it a top speed of more
than 45 knots. Johan's fish-finder was a rather more impressive affair than my
model back in England. It incorporated something like the 'sat-nav' systems
used in cars, which along with its GPS information meant that Johan was
able to take us quickly to precise locations he knew had produced big pike in
the past.

We took a bouncing, white-knuckle ride over the calm sea and visited some
of Johan's favourite bays. The pike weren't very co-operative and we struggled
to catch the occasional fish. Unruffled water, clear blue skies and a burning sun
gave us conditions that might have been perfect for a family sight-seeing
holiday but weren't ideally suited to the more important matter of catching
pike. Johan took me to a bay where his business partner had lost a very big pike
a couple of weeks previously. We fished on the drift over quite shallow water.
On Johan's advice, I was using a slow-sinking intermediate line. There was
evidence of plenty of prey-fish in the area and we started to get a little more
optimistic. On three occasions, my fly snagged on a rock and we had to back up

▲ Johan Broman's boat
on the Swedish Baltic was
an altogether sportier
craft than anything I had
previously fished from. It
was white-knuckle fast and
equipped with state of the
art GPS navigation and
positioning systems.
(Johan Broman)

▶ Johan Broman with a superb pike from the Swedish Baltic. Catching pike from the sea is a great experience. Every time you make a cast, there is the thought that the next tug could be from a pike that will give you a place in angling mythology.

the boat to retrieve it. On the fourth occasion, the rock decided to move. My rod bent over and what was clearly a very large fish started to swim around. I say 'swim around' rather than run or fight because this fish didn't seem too concerned about what was happening. I was using one of Johan's own 'Esox Lucius' fly-rods and I felt distinctly under-gunned. When this pike decided to swim underneath the boat, my usual response of applying full side-strain had no effect whatsoever. I managed to pass the line under the boat by walking around the prow with my rod tip well below the water. The trick worked and I maintained good contact with the fish. My heart was pumping away. We weren't talking but I could sense that Johan was every bit as excited as I was. This was a big pike – bigger than either of us had caught before.

Sadly, we'll never know how big. My hook pulled out. I retrieved my dishevelled fly and laid my rod down in the boat. Neither of us moved or said a word for about ten minutes. I have never felt so desolate. It was hard for either of us to summon up any enthusiasm to carry on fishing. We drank coffee. Johan made some sympathetic noises and tried to convince me it was just bad luck. I carefully checked my leader and trace and we made a couple more drifts over the same area. Johan saw a pike turn as it took a bream in the water. He estimated that it could easily have weighed more than 50 lb.

I'm sure that he will fish that spot many, many more times. I'll always be grateful for having been privileged to have fished with him. I hope that I will have the opportunity to accompany him in the future.

Sweden is a truly beautiful country. You can rent a house set in extensive forests with clear pine-scented air to fill your lungs. Swedish people enjoy the long northern days in the late spring and will welcome you with genuine hospitality. The best time to target the Baltic pike is probably May and June, although Stuart Longhurst, who runs Baltic Fly-fisher, also rates October and early November as a prime time to fish.

If you are going to fish the Baltic, it makes sense to book a guide, if only for the first few days of your trip. The Baltic redefines the expression 'big pond' but, as with all big waters, it becomes less intimidating if you tackle it in small pieces. Some very productive areas can be fished by wading but much of the fishing is best tackled with a boat. Some specialist tour operators combine self-catering accommodation with car hire, boat hire and guiding. All that you need to do is get on a plane with your tackle.

Canada

American pike fly-fishers have long regarded Canada as the ultimate location to hunt for what they term 'trophy' pike. Americans tend to measure pike by length rather than by weight. A 'trophy' fish has to be at least 42 in long. A fish this length will weigh close to 30 lb. I know anglers who have caught four such fish in a single session.

Much of the fishing involves flying from Winnipeg to more remote places. For me, the appeal of fly-fishing for pike in Canada transcends the quality of the fishing – superb as it is. It's the ultimate wilderness fishing experience. In England, I've been delighted to see the occasional otter. In Canada, you can find yourself sharing the countryside with bears. Northern Manitoba is a vast expanse of lakes, rivers and forests. Humans have had a negligible impact on this fabulous, pristine natural environment. The old adage that 'pike thrive on neglect' is emphatically illustrated by the exceptional quality of the fishing. Ireland may offer outstanding pike angling for most of the year but the short season in this northern Canadian wilderness provides the finest pike fishing I have ever experienced.

The short growing season in northern Canada means that the pike take longer to reach specimen size. An Irish pike can reach 20 lb in five years: English pike can achieve the same weight in seven years. Jason Dyck, the owner

► The transport awaits for the last leg of my journey to Northern Manitoba. A float-plane is the only realistic way of journeying into the wilderness.

► The view from the window of the float-plane shows the vast expanse of forest, lakes and rivers that form the wilderness landscape of Northern Manitoba. There is a huge amount of untapped, fabulous fishing to be explored.

of Golden Eagle Lodge on Sickle Lake in Northern Manitoba informed me that a 20 lb pike there was probably more than twenty years old. Fear not! This slower growth rate doesn't mean that the pike fail to achieve heavy-weight status. Far from it – they seem to live longer and continue growing to magnificent proportions. They fight like demons and are determined to feed actively. These factors combine to give the fly-fisherman sport of the highest quality. I have experienced the adrenalin-surging excitement of seeing four, 20 lb-plus pike in a race to be the first to nail my fly.

◀ A lithe, long, powerful pike from a Canadian lake that made the drag scream on my fly-reel. These northern pike have a short growing season and take longer to reach specimen size than their Irish or English relations. However, they survive for many years and grow to prodigious size. There is a special thrill in fishing for pike that haven't seen anyone else's fly.

You can choose to experience the Canadian adventure under canvas but you don't have to rough it. Canada boasts some superbly equipped fishing lodges. The accommodation in some of these is luxurious with top-class cuisine and excellent facilities. These lodges really do put in every effort to ensure success and enjoyment for the visiting angler.

The cost is outside many anglers' normal budget but I know many fishermen of modest means who have scrimped and saved to allow themselves to make this trip. I don't know whether they told their wives how much they had spent!

It's a short fishing season in Canada. The fishing runs from mid-June through to August. This time gives long hours of daylight and the weather is usually reliable. When the ice has melted, the big lakes can find pike in good concentrations. The angler who is in the right place can enjoy tremendous sport. The lodges provide expert guides who will help to put you in the productive areas. The best option is to make contact with one of the specialist tour operators and take their advice.

▲ Midnight on Sickle Lake. Being so far north means that the lakes of Northern Manitoba enjoy long hours of daylight in the middle of the year. I drank malt whisky and drank in the scene by a smoking fire which helped to keep the enormous, carnivorous mosquitoes at bay.

► Moose on the loose! Close encounters with the wildlife of Northern Manitoba added a special dimension to the adventure.

The cost of a trip to Canada may mean that it is a 'once in a lifetime' experience. If you are keen to sample the splendour of fishing in this magnificent country, don't fall into the trap of saying, 'One day…' and then, never getting around to it. Fly-fishing for pike is much too important to let mundane considerations like money get in the way!

Other destinations

There are many other potential destinations which can offer the adventurous angler the chance to experience the special pleasure that comes from fishing for a familiar quarry in an unfamiliar place. Every pike that I have ever caught from a new country has given me a special pleasure. Over the next few years, I intend to visit Russia and new destinations in Eastern Europe. If I travel overland, I will probably take the time to stop and, once again, enjoy some pike fishing in Holland. Despite the fact that it is such a densely populated country, there is much water to fish. Holland is also a pleasant, relaxed and civilised country. The Dutch people are unfailingly helpful and will be pleased to assist you in finding some good pike fishing.

For many years, anglers have been happy to jet off to exotic destinations to fly-fish in saltwater. Many are now waking up to the realisation that there is adventurous fishing closer to home. I have derived enormous pleasure from my travelling pike fishing and I'm looking forward to many more excursions.

Chapter 16

PRESSURE, CARE AND CONSERVATION

Pike are a superb sporting quarry and deserve our respect. We should always ensure that the pike we catch are returned to the water as quickly as possible and with the absolute minimum of stress. How we treat the pike we catch impacts on how well they fare on any water. A water which produces good pike fishing is a precious resource which needs to be nurtured and protected. There is an old (and very accurate) expression which says 'pike thrive on neglect'. Of course, as keen pike fly-fishers, we are striving to pay them as much attention as possible. This means that we should be acutely aware that our efforts can, inevitably, contribute to a decline in the quality of the fishing.

Pike don't like being caught. I am aware that I have had repeat captures of fish over the years. On a couple of occasions, I have caught a pike twice on the same day. Whilst repeat captures do happen, I feel that they are less common than with other species. I have a sizeable collection of other anglers' flies that I have removed from trout that I have caught. I know that on some waters, individual carp are caught on so many occasions that their captors give them names. To be honest, the idea of fishing for 'Priscilla the peerless pike' would have no appeal whatsoever. I like to think that when I connect with a pike, there is every chance that I am the first angler to have done so.

Catching pike has various consequences. Some pike die as a result of being caught. Sometimes, this is obvious. A few years ago, my young son Sebastian

▲ When I fished in Northern Manitoba, I was impressed with the guides' landing cradles. These supported a pike along its entire length and were kinder than a conventional landing net (they also stowed neatly on the boat). They had calibrated poles which enabled you to measure a pike easily.

caught a 10 lb pike which was hooked in the gill-rakers. It did swim off on release but was bleeding quite badly. (I realise that I should probably have knocked it on the head but Sebastian was only 8 years old at the time and desperate to know that the pike had survived. I didn't want to deflate his growing enthusiasm, so took a decision that was different from the one I would have made had I been on my own.) I returned to the lake early the following morning and discovered the corpse of a 10 lb pike. Only recently, I had a good double-figure fish bleed to death at Eyebrook for the same reason. It spoilt what had otherwise been a wonderful day. (I was fishing with the lovely Martha Thomson and we had been treated to a spectacular lesson in catching pike by an osprey.) Fortunately, incidents of this nature are rare when we are fly-fishing. Our single, barbless hook is usually caught in the scissors whereas the lure-fishers' multiple trebles are far more likely to result in damage.

Sometimes, damage is much less obvious: the pike that is caught and released, seemingly without any problem, dies later through stress. This can happen for a variety of reasons. Probably the most common one is that the pike has been kept out of the water for too long. This can be the result of a nervous, inexperienced angler taking too much time to remove the hook. Again, this is less of a problem with a fly-fisher using a big, barbless single, than it is with a bait-fishers' treble hooks. An angler who catches a sizeable pike – particularly the first such fish – may well want a photograph as permanent evidence of this heroic success. This is perfectly understandable. A pike can be photographed quickly and with minimal stress if you have a plan in place at the outset. A shout to a fishing companion when you first hook a pike is far better than awaiting their arrival some time after the fish has been unhooked. I've also seen nervous anglers drop a lively pike that they couldn't keep hold of. A quick, commemorative photograph is far better than a staged one which involves keeping the pike out of the water for too long. One picture will suffice – you don't need a collection of shots from different perspectives.

Problems can also arise as a result of a pike being played for too long. This, again, can be the result of nervousness or inexperience. Many coarse fishers assume, quite wrongly, that a flexible fly-rod contributes to this. Believe me, the rods that I use for my pike fly-fishing allow me to exert plenty of pressure. They may go a strange shape in the process but that's the whole idea. Remember, many of these rods were designed for catching tarpon or permit. Pike should always be played as firmly and as quickly as possible. To this end, you should always use a leader that is strong enough to cope with the size of pike in the water you are fishing. There is a misconception that it is somehow more 'sporting' to fish with lighter tackle. There is nothing sporting about losing your fly

◄ The bottom of a boat is a hard surface – an unhooking mat is an essential piece of equipment when you are afloat.

in a pike's jaws or having to play a fish to a standstill before you can land it. This latter point is particularly relevant in the summer, when the oxygen levels in the water tend to be lower. Algal blooms can have a serious effect on the well-being of pike as they can significantly de-oxygenate the water. Pike are more affected by this than the carp family species. At times of low oxygen levels I have witnessed pike rising, almost like trout, and poking their heads out of the water. If low oxygen levels are a problem, the best policy is to leave the pike in peace.

Hot weather and algal blooms aside, de-oxygenation can be linked to many forms of pollution. As anglers, we have a responsibility to care for the environment. If we become aware of any problems on a water, we should inform the relevant organisation without delay to enable them to take remedial action as quickly as possible. A lake that I fish was affected by a feeder stream washing toxins from farm waste into the water. This was made evident by a fish kill at the mouth of the stream. The Environment Agency was contacted straight away and they reacted promptly, putting a cordon of oxygenating pumps across the lake. Quick action prevented what could all too easily have been a catastrophe.

How a pike is released can also have a significant bearing on its survival prospects. Simply putting it back into the water isn't good enough. A fish released in this way, particularly after a long, energy-sapping fight, may simply sink out of sight and die. Always hold a fish, supporting it in the water, until it kicks and swims off strongly. The sequence of photographs showing Andy Bowman dealing with a pike from Loch Awe demonstrates the best practice.

Landing nets should have knotless mesh, and unhooking mats should be used if there is no suitable soft, damp surface on which to lay a pike whilst the hook is being removed. Too often, I see piles of scales on the bank which are evidence of bad handling practice.

Whilst we can do our utmost to ensure that our activities cause as little damage as possible, angling pressure will always have some effect on the quality of the pike fishing. When fished for regularly, pike become educated – believe me. 'New' pike may well hit a badly cast, badly tied fly. They will not be spooked by thick, visible monofilament leaders. They may be unperturbed by the presence of a boat. However, pike are wild fish. They don't survive by being oblivious to danger. They soon learn to be wary of the vibrations given off by a heavy footfall and soon become suspicious of poorly presented terminal tackle. Pike in a lake also seem to possess a form of collective consciousness – spook a few and they all seem to learn! I'm thinking that some scientists out

OPPOSITE PAGE ▶

This sequence shows Andy Bowman dealing with a good Scottish pike.

A – Chinned and ready with a supporting hand.

B – Lifted from the water and held for a quick photograph.

C – Unhooked and ready for release – like most fly-caught pike, this fish was hooked in the scissors, which made unhooking simple and speedy.

D – The pike is supported in the water to allow her to recover.

E – She is ready to go.

F – She swims off strongly.

Jason Dyck of Golden Eagle Lodge reckons that when you land a pike, you should take a deep breath. If you need to breathe again before the pike is back in the water, you're taking too long.

there will dismiss this as woolly nonsense, but this sort of response does seem common to many species. All I can say is that fly-fishing is a mysterious pursuit that is more art than science. We anglers often discover and understand truths beyond the compass of mere theorists.

Damage to pike stocks and angling pressure taken together mean that waters will often experience distinct cycles in the quality of the pike fishing that they offer.

1. Some anglers, or a lone fisherman, discover that a water holds good pike and they enjoy good sport and successful results.

2. The word gets out.

3. Lots of anglers come to fish the water and enjoy first-class sport.

4. The pike fishing deteriorates – how far depends on the water and the degree of angling pressure.

5. People stop fishing for the pike.

6. The pike recover.

7. The process starts again.

The duration of each phase can vary, as can the degree. Some waters experience a sequence of events rather than a recurring cycle: some waters fail to reach phase 6 of the cycle.

Chew Valley Lake in Somerset is a trout reservoir that is also famous for the pike it produces. When it was first realised that the lake contained huge pike, some anglers enjoyed phenomenally good sport. The fishing now is harder than it was in its heyday. I would describe the lake as being at phase 3½ of the cycle. Hopefully, it will continue to provide rewarding pike fishing for those anglers prepared to master it. Chew Valley Lake is a relatively large water. It has a close season and, during the season, the number of boats allowed on the lake is limited. On most days, the majority of anglers on the lake will be in pursuit of trout rather than pike. Although the pike are more fished for now than they were in the past, they do have some respite from our attentions. The trout reservoirs may well offer us the chance to catch good pike as a continuous, long term proposition. For part of each year, they are closed to angling. For the majority of the time that they are open, the rules specify that anglers can only fly-fish. This means that the venues are not subject to significant, constant pressure from bait fishermen. I realise that I risk being accused of an elitist attitude – but long may this continue.

Some smaller waters, such as gravel pits of fifty acres or less, go through the whole cycle every five years or so. Some big pike are caught; the word gets out and suddenly the banks are surrounded by bait-fishers' 'bivvies'. Fly-fishing becomes pointless as all the productive stretches of bank are 'staked out' by anglers prepared to fish for several days (and sometimes nights as well) in succession, determined to add to their tally of specimen pike.

Some waters never recover. If the big, dominant pike at the top of the food pyramid die, the result can be an explosion in the small pike population. Big pike are the most effective culling mechanism of their smaller relatives. They are an important component in a finely tuned system which ensures the maintenance of a permanently healthy balance between prey-fish and predators. If our fishing pressure disrupts this balance, we can destroy the special set of circumstances which allowed both the pike and their prey to thrive.

As mentioned earlier in these pages, I have the good fortune to fish a classical old estate lake near my home in North Wiltshire. It is an extremely fertile water which is neither artificially stocked nor actively managed. There has been a perfect and ongoing balance between the pike, which grow to prodigious size, and the abundant prey-fish, which thrive. The lake is fished by a club which has restricted membership and operates the old coarse fishing close season. In addition – and perhaps more importantly – more than half of the lake is 'out of bounds' and is not fished. This means that the pike have a refuge in terms of both time and space. Certainly, it can be frustrating to know that at times the pike are in the deeper water, in the part of the lake that I can't fish, but my frustration is borne stoically. Every year, for many years, I have caught several 20 lb pike from this water. Most years someone (sometimes myself) catches a pike of more than 30 lb. In the opening week of the 2007 season, I caught two 20 lb pike and several big doubles, and my guiding clients (one per day for four days) also caught three 20 lb pike and many big doubles. The consistent, high quality of the pike fishing on this lake has been protected by the Estate's policy of restricting the pressure that the pike are subjected to – long may it continue. In these times when the money god is worshipped by many devotees, it is inspiring to find that some country landowners put environmental preservation above financial profit. Lord Lansdowne will always have my respect and gratitude for this.

England is a small country with a large population and a limited amount of water. People now have the ability to travel and to fish throughout the land. If we in this country want to be able to enjoy our wonderful sport in the future, we need to adopt a caring and protective attitude to both our quarry and to the fascinating environment they live in. Other countries have a lower population density and more water. Whilst places such as Canada and Ireland may have more capacity to cope with the pressure we humans put on our environment, they are not immune and areas that are too heavily fished can suffer.

▶ Many anglers who target other species think that pike should be removed to allow the other fish to thrive. Pike don't devour their food supply but rather (if we don't meddle with nature) they find a balance which benefits the whole aquatic environment. The best control of the pike population is the big female pike at the top of the pyramid.

It's worth bearing in mind that pike have evolved to be the top predators in their own aquatic environment. They haven't evolved to cope with serious interference from humans. Nowadays, if I have caught a few pike, I will normally bring my session to a close, happy that I have enjoyed some success. This self-restraint has become easier to practice as my fly-rod has caught more pike! I also find myself increasingly keen to fish less-known waters that aren't thronged by other anglers. I do appreciate that I am in a fortunate position here, as I am able to devote a substantial amount of time into researching and exploring new waters. However, as fly-fishermen, we should be concerned with more than simply catching lots of pike. Rather than imposing ourselves onto the natural environment, we should strive to connect with it. If we can feel part of the great scheme of nature, we will value and protect it rather than abuse it.

USEFUL CONTACTS

These contacts are listed in broad categories. As you will see, a number of them can provide a range of complementary services.

Guiding/boat hire/casting instruction

Broman, Johan Fly-rod designer, guide with boat, expert Baltic pike angler.
EMAIL – johanbroman@telia.com
TELEPHONE – 0046 8 540 68033

Funke, Bodo Guiding and boat hire, based in County Roscommon, Ireland.
EMAIL – info@anglingservicesireland.com
WEBSITE – www.anglingservicesireland.com
TELEPHONE – 00353 71 9663580

Gaunt-Baker, Tim Casting instruction, guiding, based in Norfolk, England.
TELEPHONE – 0044 1553 813769

Hendrick, Jim Guiding and boat hire in Ireland. Jim is also an expert saltwater fly-fishing guide for bass.
TELEPHONE – 00353 53 9123351

Jackson, Terry Guide with boat, based in Northern Ireland but knowledgeable throughout Ireland.
TELEPHONE – 0044 284 2738120

Lafforgue, Xavier Guiding, boat hire and B&B, based in County Monaghan, Ireland.
TELEPHONE – 00353 42 9663207

Smith, Andy Casting instruction, guiding, based in Nottinghamshire, England.
EMAIL – andy.smith@fishconsulting.net
TELEPHONE – 0044 115 9394002

Wolsoncroft-Dodds, David Guiding, instruction, custom-tied flies, courses and hosted trips. I'm happy to provide whatever assistance I can to the budding pike fly-fisher.
EMAIL – david@flyfishforpike.co.uk
WEBSITE – www.flyfishforpike.co.uk
BLOG – dwdodds.blogspot.com
TELEPHONE – 0044 1249 890114

Travel advice, arrangements and accommodation

Central Fisheries Board Information about fishing throughout Ireland. The Angling Advisor, Mark Corps, is an accomplished pike fly-fisher.
EMAIL – mark.corps@cfb.ie
WEBSITE – www.cfb.ie

Go Fishing Worldwide Organise pike fly-fishing trips to the Baltic and to wonderful venues in Canada.
EMAIL – maggi@gofishingworldwide.co.uk
WEBSITE – www.gofishingworldwide.co.uk
TELEPHONE – 0044 208 742 1556

Longhurst, Stuart Runs Baltic Fly-fisher; can arrange guided fishing on the Baltic.
EMAIL – stuart@balticflyfisher.com
WEBSITE – www.balticflyfisher.com
TELEPHONE – 0049 4182 291312

Melview Lodge Accommodation in Longford, Ireland. Host, Kevin Lyons, is extremely knowledgeable about pike fishing venues in the surrounding area and can supply boats. He can also arrange for a guide and can organise hosted trips.
EMAIL – info@melviewlodge.com
WEBSITE – www.melviewlodge.com
TELEPHONE – 00353 434 5061

Stena Line Ferry company operating services between Britain and Ireland.
WEBSITE – www.stenaline.co.uk

Tourism Ireland Information about accommodation in Ireland.
WEBSITE – www.discoverireland.com

Suppliers of specialist pike-fly materials

Carrilon A fly-fishing tackle dealership that is making genuine efforts to cater fully for the pike fly-fisher.
EMAIL – rob@carrilon.com
WEBSITE – www.carrilon.com
TELEPHONE – 0044 1302 719933

Enrico Puglisi Manufacturer of fly-tying materials
EMAIL – enrico@epflies.com
Website – www.epflies.com

U.K. Saltwater Flies Proprietor Austen Goldsmith stocks a wide range of fly-tying materials suitable for pike.
EMAIL – sales@uksaltwaterflies.com
TELEPHONE – 0044 1326 562753

Clubs and associations

The Pike Anglers Club of Great Britain They promote care and conservation of pike. Whilst the majority of their members are bait or lure anglers, we are all fishing for the same quarry and can learn much about pike from one another.
Website – www.pacgb.com

The Pike Fly-fishing Association A club based in England. They organise fishing days on top venues.
WEBSITE – www.pffa.co.uk

Recommended reading

Reynolds, Barry and John Berryman, *Pike on the Fly*, Spring Creek Press, USA.

Swier, Ad, *Passion for Pike*, Westerlaan Publisher, Lichtenvoorde, Holland.

INDEX